CONTENTS

underlined chapters are in summer exam

Introduction — vi

Introduction	vi ☐
Exam Section	vii ☐

Unit 1 — 1

1 The Scientific Method and Experiments	1 ☑
2 The Characteristics of Life	5 ☑
3 Food	7 ☐
4 Ecology Theory	12 ☐
5 Human Impact on an Ecosystem	24 ☐
6 Study of an Ecosystem	27 ☐

Unit 2 — 34

7 Cell Structure	34 ☐
8 Cell Diversity	39 ☐
9 Enzymes	43 ☐
10 Photosynthesis	52 ☐
11 Respiration	60 ☐
12 Diffusion and Osmosis	67 ☐
13 Cell Division	71 ☐
14 Genetics	77 ☐
15 DNA and RNA	90 ☐
16 Evolution	100 ☐
17 Genetic Engineering	103 ☐

Unit 3		107
18 The Five Kingdoms	107	☐
19 Monera	109	☐
20 Fungi	116	☐
21 *Amoeba*	121	☐
22 The Structure of Flowering Plants	122	☐
23 Transport, Storage and Gas Exchange in Flowering Plants	127	☐
24 Blood	131	☐
25 The Human Defence System	135	☐
26 The Heart and Blood Vessels	141	☐
27 The Lymphatic System	149	☐
28 Animal Nutrition	151	☐
29 Homeostasis and Excretion	158	☐
30 Human Breathing	165	☐
31 The Nervous System	170	☐
32 The Senses	177	☐
33 The Endocrine System	182	☐
34 Human Reproduction	187	☐
35 Plant Responses	201	☐
36 The Skeleton and Muscles	208	☐
37 Viruses	214	☐
38 Sexual Reproduction in Flowering Plants	217	☐
39 Vegetative Propagation	228	☐
Index	**231**	
Study Guide	**235**	

Studied for Exam on the 9/11/17.

Experiments

1   To test food for starch, reducing sugar, protein and lipid   8,9

2   To collect flora and fauna   28

3   Using a key to identify flora and fauna   29

4a Using a quadrat to conduct a quantitative study of plants   30

4b Using the capture/recapture method to conduct a quantitative
    study of animals   31

5   To measure three abiotic factors in a habitat   31

6   To use a light microscope   35

7   To examine plant and animal cells under a microscope   35,36

8   To investigate the effect of pH on the rate of enzyme action   46

9   To investigate the effect of temperature on the rate of enzyme activity   47

10 To investigate the denaturation of an enzyme by heat   48

11 To prepare an enzyme immobilisation and examine its application   50,51

12 To investigate the influence of light intensity or carbon dioxide
    concentration on the rate of photosynthesis   54

13 To prepare and show the production of alcohol by yeast   65

14 To demonstrate osmosis   68

15 To isolate DNA from a plant tissue   92

16 To investigate the growth of leaf yeasts   119

17 To prepare and examine microscopically a transverse section (TS)
    of a dicot stem   126

18 To dissect, display and identify a sheep (or ox) heart   144

19a* To investigate the effect of exercise on the pulse rate   148

19b* To investigate the effect of exercise on the rate of breathing   168

20 To investigate the effect of IAA on plant tissue   205

21 To investigate the effects of water, oxygen and temperature on
    germination   226

22 To show digestive action during germination   227

*Note: You can choose to do either 19a or 19b

Introduction

The Leaving Cert Biology course is divided into three units. Unit 1 is very short, Unit 3 comprises about half the course, while Unit 2 makes up the rest of the course.

In this book Chapters 1 to 6 cover Unit 1, Chapters 7 to 17 cover Unit 2 and Chapters 18 to 39 cover Unit 3.

The Leaving Cert Biology course is recognised as being a very long course. This book attempts to provide a short, concise account of the entire course. The information provided is based on:

- The syllabus and guidelines
- The contents of previous Leaving Certificate examinations.

The language used is straightforward and to the point. Diagrams and flowcharts have been included where relevant. Key definitions are highlighted and many Remember, Top Tip and Point to Note boxes are provided to help reinforce learning.

Fertilisation is the union of the male and female gametes.

> **Point to note**
>
> The course requires that you know of any one practice of conservation from the areas of agriculture, fisheries or forestry.

Key definition   A point to remember

In many parts of the course a choice is available. These choices are clearly identified to avoid confusion with the options given in different textbooks.

The 22 mandatory practical activities are all included. They are located in various chapters so that they are integrated with the theory of each activity.

Relationship between units and questions asked

The number of questions on the final paper based on each unit is given below.

Unit	Number of questions	
	Section A (short questions)	Section C (long questions)
1	2	1
2	2	2
3	2	3

The practical activities are examined in section B of the paper where three questions are based on these activities. However, practical work is often also asked in parts of sections A and C.

Study Guide

The Study Guide on **p.235** will help you to keep track of your revision.

- Work out how much time you have left before the exam and how much time you can devote to each chapter.
- Try to be realistic when setting your targets.
- Tick off the boxes as you meet your goals.
- Re-evaluate your plan if you feel you have been over ambitious.
- In the days before the exam, check that you have covered all key areas.
- Remember that about 25% of the marks are given for definitions and another 25% are given for the experiments. Make sure you know your definitions and the 22 experiments on the course.

Exam section

The following table shows the layout of the Leaving Certificate Biology examination:

Section	Number of questions asked	Number of questions to be attempted	Marks per question	Marks for this section	Percentage for this section
A	6	5	20	100	25
B	3	2	30	60	15
C	6	4	60	240	60

In sections A and B the answers are filled into the spaces provided. In section C the answers are written into an answer booklet.

Three hours are allocated for the examination. Most students can complete the exam in this time. However, the following table provides a suggested time frame for the exam.

Section	Time (in minutes)	Time per question
A	30	6
B	20	10
C	120	30

These suggestions allow ten minutes for reading over the entire paper before the exam or for tidying up at the end of the exam.

Exam paper analysis chart

Topics that have appeared in previous Leaving Cert Higher Level Biology papers

Topics asked at Higher Level	2004	2005	2006	2007	2008	2009	2010	2011	2012	2013	2014
The Scientific Method		2			3		8	7		9(a)	9
The Characteristics of Life											
Food		1	7	1	1	1	1, 8	1	1	1	2
Ecology Theory	10	12 (a), (b)	2, 10(a)	2, 12	10 (a), (b)	3, 11	5, 12	3, 10(b)	11(a), (b)	2, 7(a), 15	1, 15
Pollution, Conservation and Waste	5		10(c)		10(c)	11(a)			4		15(c)
Study of an Ecosystem		12(c)	9, 10(b)		7	11(c)		10(c)	11(c)	7(b)	
Cell Structure			8				8	14(c)	12(a)	9(b)	8
Cell Diversity							4		2		
Enzymes		7	3	7, 11(c)	9	9	14(b)	14(b)	9	8	13
Photosynthesis	11	4	11	9	14(a)	12(c)	8, 14(a)	14(a)	12(b)	9(b), 14(a)	
Respiration	7	11	4	11 (a), (b)	5	12(a), (b)		6	12(c)	14(b), (c)	6, 13(c)
Diffusion and Osmosis					14(c)		14(c)	14(c)	15(c)	5, 9(b)	
Cell Division		5		3	2	5		2		11(c)	5
DNA and RNA	13	8	7	10	14(b)						10(a), (b)
Genetic Crosses	3	10(b), (c)	12(b)	5	11	10(a), (b)	8, 10(a), (b)	9	10(a)	6	10(c)
Evolution	2		12(a), (c)			10(c)	2, 10(c)	13(b), (c)	10(b)	11(b)	
Genetic Engineering						6		13(a)	6	11(a)	
Classification of Organisms									10(c)		4
Monera	15(c)	15(b)	15(b)	14(b)	15(c)		15(c)(ii)				
Fungi		9, 15(c)		8		14(c)		15(c)	8, 14(c)	12(b)	
Protista							3				
Structure of Flowering Plants	8		14(c)	6	14(c)	7			5		14(b)

Transport, Food Storage and Gas Exchange in Flowering Plants	4	3(a), 14(a)	6(a), 11(c)		14(a)			15 (b)			12(a), 14(c)
Blood			13(a)	13(a)(ii)		13(b)			15(b)		
The Heart and Blood Vessels	9		5(a)(b)	13(a)	13(a)(ii)	13(a) (b)	7				9, 12(c)
The Lymphatic System			13(c)								3
Human Nutrition	6		3(a), (b), (c), 5		12		15(b), 15(c) (iii)	5	15(a)		
Homeostasis	12(a)			15(c)		15(c)			15(c)	3	
Human Breathing				13(b), (c)		13(c)					9, 12(b), (c)
Excretion	12(b), (c)	3(a)	13(b)	15(c)	13		15(c)(iv), (v)	4, 12	15(c)		
Plant Responses	15(b)	14(b)	6(d), 7		8	2	9	11(a), (b)		10(c)	
The Nervous System	15(a)	3(b), 14(c)	14(b)		4	15(c)	11(a), (b)		13		11(b),(c)
The Senses			14(c)			15(b)		15(a)		10(a), (b)	
The Endocrine System		14(c)		15(b)	15(a)	4	11(c)	11(c)			
The Skeleton and Muscles		3(d)							3		11(a)
The Human Defence System		15(a)	6(e)	14(c)		15(c)			15(b)	12(c)	
Viruses		15(a)		14(b)	15(b)	15(c)	6			12(a)	
Sexual Reproduction in Flowering Plants	14(a)	3(g), (j)	14(a)	14(a)		8, 15(c)	13		14(a), 7(b)	9(b)	7, 14(a)
Vegetative Propagation						15(a)				4	
Human Reproduction	14(b), (c)	13	15(c)	4, 15(a)	6	14(a), (b)	15(a), 15(c) (i)		14(b)	13	

Topics that have appeared in previous Leaving Cert Higher Level Biology papers

Experiments asked at Higher Level	2004	2005	2006	2007	2008	2009	2010	2011	2012	2013	2014
Food Tests		1(d)	7		1(e)		8	1, 8			
Ecology											
Using a Key			9					10(c)		7(b)	
Ecology Collection											
Quantitative Study in Ecology		12(c)	9, 10(b)			11(c)		10(c)	11(c)	7(b)	
Measuring Abiotic Factors in Ecology					7					7(b)	
Microscope											
Use of a Microscope			8								8
To Examine Plant or Animal Cells Using a Microscope			8				8			9(b)	8
To Prepare and Examine a TS of a Dicot Stem	8		14(c)			7		8			
Enzymes											
pH and Enzyme Activity											
Temperature and Enzyme Activity				7					9		
Heat Denaturation on Enzyme Activity					9					8	
Enzyme Immobilisation and its Application						9				14(c)	
Effect of Light Intensity or Carbon Dioxide Concentration on Photosynthesis	11(c)			9		12(c)	8	14(a)		9(b)	

Experiment									
To Prepare and Show the Production of Alcohol by Yeast	7								13(c)
To Demonstrate Osmosis	11(c)			14(c)			14(c)		9(b)
To Isolate DNA from a Plant Tissue	8	7	10(c)			8	9	8	
To Investigate the Growth of Leaf Yeast	9		8			8	8	8	9
To Dissect, Display and Identify the Parts of a Heart			9			7			
To Investigate the Effects of Exercise on Pulse Rate or Breathing Rate						8	8		9
To Investigate the Effects of IAA on Plant Tissue		7		8		9			
Germination									
To Investigate the Effects of Water, Oxygen and Temperature on Germination		7							
To Use Starch Agar or Skimmed Milk Plates to Show Digestive Action During Germination		7			8			9(b)	7

Exam techniques

Section A and B

- Answer these sections using a good-quality HB pencil (or an erasable pen). This allows you to rewrite an answer if it is wrong or if it is too long to fit into the spaces provided.
- Keep your answers short and make sure they fit into the spaces provided. Practising answering these questions is the best way to achieve this.
- Answer all the questions asked if you can; i.e. in Section A, answer all six questions and in Section B, answer all three questions. You will be marked on your best answers.
- If possible, answer all parts of each question; you may get some marks if your answer has any correct information in it.
- Recheck your answers to Question 1 when you have finished Section A. It is common to make basic errors in the first few minutes of an exam due to lack of concentration.

Section C

Although this section has longer questions than the other two sections there is a growing trend for the questions in Section C to require short, snappy answers similar to Sections A and B.

- Read each question slowly and thoroughly. Think carefully about the question (not your answer at this stage). Does the question ask you to describe, suggest, distinguish, list, give an outline account, etc? Are diagrams asked for (or is it just a single diagram)? Focus on the question before rushing in to provide an answer.
- Some students find it helpful to highlight parts of the question using a highlighter or a red pen. This helps them to focus on the question.
- Answer exactly what is asked in the question. For example:
    - If you are asked about the events in Stage 1 of respiration you will get no marks for writing about Stage 2.
    - If the question asks for a labelled diagram, you will lose marks if the correct diagram is not drawn and labelled.
    - If the question asks you to **distinguish** between the light stage and the dark stage of photosynthesis, you need only one or two sentences to give a major difference between them.
    - If the question asks you to **describe** the light stage and the dark stage of photosynthesis, you need a much longer account of each of them.
    - If the question asks for the precise location of the production of blood cells, the answer 'bone marrow' will not get full marks (as it is not precise enough); you have to answer 'the bone marrow of bones such as the femur and sternum'.

- If the question asks for groups of materials carried in the blood, answers such as 'oxygen' and 'glucose' are not correct, as they are not groups of materials. Correct answers would be 'gases', 'foods', 'salts', 'wastes' and 'hormones'.

- Look out for plurals in the question. For example, does it ask 'State a reason ...' or 'State reasons ...'? Does the question start with 'Describe with the aid of a diagram ... ' or 'Describe with the aid of diagrams ... '?

- Answer an extra question if time allows, i.e. answer five questions instead of four. You will be marked on your best four answers.

- In Questions 14 and 15 you are given parts (a), (b) and (c) and asked to attempt any two parts. It is acceptable to attempt all three parts. You will be allocated marks for the best two parts.

- Diagrams should:
  - Be drawn with an HB pencil
  - Be large (about the size of your fist)
  - Have a title
  - Be fully labelled (include as many labels as you can)
  - Be realistic in their shape and proportions.

Common mistakes

- Failing to answer the required number of questions.
- Failing to answer all parts of a question (to prevent this happening in Section C some students cross out the part of the question they have just completed).
- Failing to read the question carefully enough.
- Not answering exactly what the question asked.
- Failing to practise on past and sample papers.
- Not relating your answers to the marking schemes, which are available at www.examinations.ie

UNIT 1

The Scientific Method and Experiments   1

Learning objectives

In this chapter you will learn about:

1 The scientific method
2 Theories and principles
3 The limits of the value of the scientific method
4 Experiments

The scientific method

The scientific method is the way in which knowledge of the physical world is obtained.

The main steps in the scientific method are:

① Observing

We notice something in the world around us and begin to ask questions about it. Our observations cause us to become curious.

② Forming a hypothesis

A *hypothesis* is a best guess based on our observations. The hypothesis tries to explain our observations. A hypothesis may be true, partly true, or it may be false.

③ Carrying out an experiment

An *experiment* is a test for a hypothesis. One or more experiments are carried out to test if the hypothesis is true, partly true, or false. Experiments are the basis of the scientific method.

④ Forming a conclusion

Data is the information gathered in an experiment.

Data, which is the unprocessed information obtained in an experiment, is collected. The data is analysed and processed to provide results. Depending on the result, a conclusion is formed.

Relating the conclusion to the hypothesis

The results of the experiment(s) may support, reject or change the original hypothesis. If the hypothesis is changed a new hypothesis is formed and then tested by carrying out a new experiment.

Theories and principles

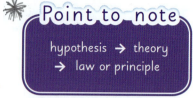

Point to note

hypothesis → theory → law or principle

When a hypothesis has been supported by many experiments over long periods of time, it forms a theory. A *theory* is a hypothesis that is supported by experiments. A theory is more likely to be true than a hypothesis. If a theory can be proven to be true over a long time and under all conditions, it takes on the status of a principle or law. A principle or law is a theory that is supported by many experiments.

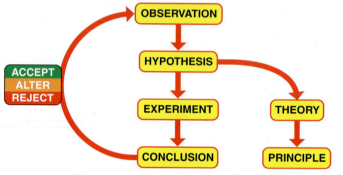

Summary of the scientific method

The limits of the value of the scientific method

The extent of our knowledge

The scientific method is based on making observations and asking questions. These questions arise from our existing knowledge. If we knew more about something, we would ask more questions and make more progress.

The basis of investigation

If there is a flaw in an experiment, any findings arising from this experiment are invalid. It is often difficult to design perfect experiments or to have an ideal control.

Ability to interpret results

It is often difficult to see how the results of an experiment relate to the original hypothesis.

Changes in the natural world

Life is constantly changing or evolving. This means that scientific findings must be constantly revised to allow for changes in the living world.

Accidental discoveries

Although the scientific method is based on findings that emerge from planned experiments, it is often the case that new discoveries and thinking may emerge from accidental discoveries.

Experiments

For experiments to be valid they must be carried out using the following agreed rules.

Experimental design

Each experiment must be designed so that only one factor (or variable) is being tested.

Safety

The safety of the experimenter(s) and others must always be a major consideration. Each experiment carries its own safety requirements.

Control experiment

A *control* is a comparison for the actual experiment. A control should have only one difference (or variable) compared to the actual experiment.

Point to note

a control = a comparison

If there is a difference between the results of the actual experiment and the control, the difference can be associated with the one factor that was varied or changed.

Sample size

It is important to carry out experiments on as large a sample as possible. If a single plant, animal, cell or other sample is tested, the result may be due to factors associated with just that single item.

In general, the larger the sample size the more valid the results.

Random selection

When selecting a sample to be tested it is best to select the items at random. This eliminates the chance of a biased or unfair selection.

Replication

A *replicate* is a repeated experiment. The results of a single experiment do not carry much weight in the context of the scientific method.

To be fully accepted each experiment is reported in scientific journals or on the World Wide Web. This allows the experiment to be repeated (or replicated).

Double-blind testing

A *double-blind* test means that neither the person carrying out the experiment nor the person on whom the experiment is carried out knows who is in the actual experiment or who is part of the control group.

Double-blind testing prevents the person who is carrying out the experiment from unconsciously influencing the results.

The Characteristics of Life   2

Learning objectives

In this chapter you will learn about:

1 The definition of life
2 The characteristics of life
3 Metabolism
4 Continuity of life

The definition of life

There is no satisfactory and fully acceptable definition of life. However, the following definition is commonly accepted.

Life is the possession of all five of the following features: organisation, nutrition, excretion, reproduction and response (or behaviour).

The characteristics of life

1 ***Organisation* means that living things are organised into cells.**
   Cells in turn form tissues (groups of cells with the same function), organs (a number of tissues combine to form an organ), organ systems (consisting of a number of organs) and individual organisms (an organism is a living thing).

2 ***Nutrition* is the way in which organisms obtain and use food.**
   Plants make their own food in the process of photosynthesis. Animals obtain their food by feeding on other organisms.

3 ***Excretion* is the removal of the waste products of chemical reactions.**
   Excretion helps organisms to maintain a fairly constant balance between their internal and external environments.

4 ***Reproduction* is the production of new individuals.**
   Living things arise from other living things by the process of reproduction.

5 ***Response* means that living things react to changes (called stimuli) in their surroundings.**
   Animals have well-developed sense organs and nervous systems that allow them to respond to stimuli such as light, sound, smell, touch and taste. Plants

> **Point to note**
>
> ONERR stands for Organisation, Nutrition, Excretion, Reproduction and Response.

respond more slowly than animals. They respond by changing their growth towards or away from stimuli such as light, temperature and water in the soil.

Metabolism

Metabolism is the sum of all the chemical reactions in an organism.

Metabolism includes reactions such as digestion of food, speed of repair, production of new cells, production of energy (in respiration) and photosynthesis.

Continuity of life

Continuity of life means that living things arise from other living things.

Food

3

Learning objectives

In this chapter you will learn about:

1 The elements in food

2 Carbohydrates

3 Proteins

4 Lipids

5 Vitamins

6 Minerals

7 Anabolism and catabolism

The elements in food

Food contains 14 chemical elements. These elements join together to form four main types of food biomolecules: carbohydrates, lipids, proteins and vitamins. **Biomolecules are chemicals made by living things.**

- The six most common elements in food are carbon, hydrogen, oxygen, nitrogen, phosphorus and sulfur.
- Five elements found dissolved in salts are sodium, magnesium, chlorine, potassium and calcium.
- Three elements found in trace (tiny) amounts are iron, copper and zinc.

Carbohydrates

Structure and types of carbohydrates

Carbohydrates contain the elements carbon, hydrogen and oxygen. These elements are present in the ratio $C_x(H_2O)_y$, where x and y are the same number. For example, glucose has the formula $C_6H_{12}O_6$.

There are three categories of carbohydrates:

- *Monosaccharides* **consist of one sugar unit.** Examples include glucose, fructose and ribose.
- *Disaccharides* **are made of two sugar units joined together.** Examples are maltose (glucose + glucose) and sucrose or table sugar (glucose + fructose).

- ***Polysaccharides* are made of many sugar units joined together.** Examples include starch (stored by plants and found in flour, bread, potatoes, rice, pasta), cellulose (plant cell walls, forms roughage or fibre in our diet), glycogen (stored by animals in the liver and muscles).

Functions of carbohydrates

- Structural function: cellulose forms cell walls.
- Metabolic functions: glucose gives energy in respiration; glycogen stores energy in animals; starch stores energy in plants.

 Experiment

To test food for starch

1   Add a few drops of iodine (a red/yellow colour) to the food.
2   A blue-black colour shows that starch is present.
3   **Control** = add iodine to water (to get a red/yellow colour).

To test food for reducing (or simple) sugar

1   Dissolve a sample of the food in water.
2   Add a few drops of Benedict's (or Fehling's I and II) solution. Both of these are blue.
3   Heat in a boiling water bath for a few minutes.
4   If the colour turns red, reducing sugar is present.
5   **Control** = add Benedict's (or Fehling's I and II) solution to water (to get a blue colour).

Proteins

Structure of proteins

- Proteins always contain the elements carbon, hydrogen, oxygen and nitrogen. Some proteins contain sulfur, phosphorus and other elements.
- These elements combine to form amino acids, which are the basic building blocks of proteins. Amino acids combine in increasing numbers to form peptides, polypeptides and proteins.
- To allow them to function properly many proteins are folded into complex three-dimensional shapes.

Sources of protein

Meat, fish, eggs, milk, peas and beans are good sources of protein.

Functions of proteins

- Structural functions: keratin is found in hair and skin; myosin is found in muscles.
- Metabolic functions: enzymes control reactions; antibodies fight infections.

Experiment

To test food for protein (the Biuret test)

1   Dissolve the food in water.

2   Add sodium hydroxide (colourless) and copper sulfate (blue). These two chemicals form Biuret solution.

3   If the colour turns purple or violet, protein is present.

4   **Control** = add Biuret solution to water (to get a blue colour).

Lipids

Structure of lipids

- Lipids contain the elements carbon, hydrogen and oxygen only.
- Lipids include fats (which are solid at room temperature) and oils (liquid at room temperature).
- The basic unit of lipids is a triglyceride. Each triglyceride is composed of a single glycerol to which three fatty acids are attached.
- Phospholipids are fatty substances in which a phosphate group replaces one of the fatty acid groups.

Sources of lipids

Foods rich in lipids include butter, cream, milk, meat, oils and fried food.

Functions of lipids

- Provide energy
- Store energy (they contain twice as much energy as the equivalent weight of carbohydrate or protein)
- Phospholipids form part of cell membranes.

Experiment

To test food for lipid (or fat)

1   Rub a sample of the food on brown paper.

2   If a permanent stain appears (which will not dry out), lipid or fat is present.

3   **Control** = rub water on brown paper (no permanent stain will form).

Vitamins

Water-soluble vitamin

Vitamin C is a vitamin that dissolves in water.

Sources

Fruits (such as oranges, lemons, limes, blackcurrants) and vegetables are sources of vitamin C.

Use

Vitamin C is needed to form skin, gums, cartilage, ligaments and blood vessels.

Deficiency

A deficiency (or shortage) of vitamin C results in a disease called scurvy. Symptoms (or signs) of scurvy include poor healing of skin, bruising and poor gums with loose teeth.

Fat-soluble vitamin

Vitamin D dissolves in fat but not in water.

Sources

Liver, fish oils and milk; vitamin D is also made when ultraviolet rays in sunlight act on our skin.

Use

Vitamin D is needed to absorb calcium from our intestines into the blood.

Deficiency

A lack of vitamin D causes rickets in children and osteomalacia in adults. Both disorders result in weak, brittle bones.

Minerals

Minerals needed by plants include:

- Calcium, which is needed to hold cell walls together.
- Magnesium, which is used to make the green pigment, chlorophyll.

Minerals needed by animals include:

- Calcium, which forms bones and teeth.
- Iron, which forms the pigment haemoglobin in red blood cells.

The importance of water for living things

1   It is a major component of cytoplasm and body fluids.

2   It is a good solvent. This means that many molecules can dissolve in water. This allows many cell reactions to take place. It also allows the molecules to be transported.

3   Water plays a key role in many chemical reactions. For example, it is needed in photosynthesis and is produced in respiration.

4   It is easy for water to pass in or out of biological membranes. This means that water can easily enter and leave cells and cell parts such as mitochondria and chloroplasts.

5   Water has a high specific heat capacity. This means that water is a good absorber of heat and is difficult to warm up or to cool down. As a result, organisms living in water or mainly composed of water tend to have stable temperatures. This allows their reactions to take place at constant rates.

Anabolism and catabolism

Anabolic reactions make larger molecules from smaller ones.

Anabolic reactions (such as photosynthesis or making protein from amino acids) require energy to take place.

Catabolic reactions break down larger molecules to form smaller ones.

Catabolic reactions (such as respiration or the breakdown of carbohydrates, proteins or fats) release energy.

4 Ecology Theory

Learning objectives

In this chapter you will learn about:

1 Ecological definitions
2 Factors affecting organisms
3 Energy flow
4 Pyramid of numbers
5 Niche
6 Nutrient recycling
7 Population control
8 Population dynamics
9 Human population numbers

Ecological definitions

- *Ecology* **is the study of the interactions between living things and between living things and their environment.**

- **The *biosphere* is that part of the Earth containing living organisms.**

  The biosphere includes the air, soil and rock, and the oceans.

- **An *ecosystem* is a group of organisms that interact with each other and with their environment.** The Earth is itself one large ecosystem. This global ecosystem is called the biosphere. The biosphere is divided into many smaller ecosystems. Each ecosystem contains similar climate, soil and organisms such as plants and animals.

  Examples of ecosystems include rainforests, deserts, grasslands and seashores.

- **A *habitat* is the place where an organism lives.** An ecosystem is too large to study as an entire unit. The local area that we study is called a habitat.

> ### Top Tips!
>
> You are required to study **one** type of ecosystem.
>
> This book will deal with a grassland ecosystem.

Factors affecting organisms

The types (and numbers) of organisms living in an ecosystem or habitat depend on four categories of factors.

- Environmental factors
- Climatic factors
- Edaphic factors
- Aquatic factors

Environmental factors

Environmental factors can be considered as abiotic or biotic.

Abiotic factors **are non-living features of the environment.** Examples of some abiotic factors are:

Factor	Example
Aspect (the direction a surface is facing)	Plants grow better on south-facing aspects.
Exposure (to wind, sunlight, currents or drying out)	There is less light under a tree and so fewer plants grow in the shade of a tree or hedge.
Soil pH	Different plants are suited to different soil pHs.
Climatic and edaphic factors	Dealt with later in this chapter.

Biotic **factors are living factors.** Examples of some biotic factors are:

Factor	Example
Food	The more plants in a habitat, the more animals can live there.
Competition (for scarce resources)	Competition tends to reduce the numbers of organisms.
Predation (catching and eating prey)	Predation tends to reduce the numbers of prey.
Parasitism (feeding from a live host)	Parasitism may reduce the numbers of the host organism.

Climatic factors

Climate **is weather over a long period of time.** Examples of some climatic factors are given in the following table.

Factor	Example
Temperature	Organisms grow faster in higher temperatures.
Rainfall	All organisms need water to grow.
Light intensity	Plants and algae need light for photosynthesis.
Wind	Wind damages plants, stunts their growth and increases evaporation.

Edaphic factors

Edaphic factors relate to the soil. Examples of some edaphic factors are:

Factor	Example
Soil pH	Different plants prefer different soil pHs.
Soil type	Some plants tolerate sandy soil (large particles); others tolerate clay soil (small particles).
Humus (decaying organic matter) content	Normally increases the growth of plants.
Water, air and mineral content of the soil	Each of these increases the growth of plants.

Aquatic factors

Aquatic factors relate to organisms living in or near water-based environments. The rocky seashore is an aquatic environment (as opposed to grassland, which is a terrestrial or land-based environment).

The most important factors in terrestrial environments are often temperature and rainfall.

In aquatic environments edaphic factors do not apply. However, the following special factors are important.

Factor	Example
Light	Light may not penetrate too far down into water if it is very murky (as is the case in seawater due to sand turbulence).
Currents	Currents may wash away algae, plants and animals.
Wave action	Waves create currents and physically damage organisms.
Oxygen concentration	There is much less oxygen in water than there is in air.

Energy flow

All ecosystems need an external supply of energy in order to function. The Sun (solar energy) is the main source of energy for the Earth and its ecosystems.

Solar energy is converted into food (by algae and plants) in photosynthesis.

Flora means plants and algae. Fauna means animals. Feeding allows energy to pass from flora to fauna.

Food chain

A grazing food chain is the simplest way to represent the flow of energy in an ecosystem.

A *food chain* is a sequence of organisms in which each organism is eaten by the next one in the chain.

Examples of grazing food chains are:

Grass → Rabbit → Fox

Dandelion → Snail → Thrush → Hawk

Point to note

The arrows show the direction in which the energy flows.

- A grazing food chain always starts with a producer. **A producer is an organism that makes its own food.**
- The producer is eaten by a primary consumer. **A consumer is an organism that takes its food from another organism.**
- The primary consumer is a herbivore. **A herbivore is an organism that feeds on flora.**
- The primary consumers are eaten by secondary consumers. These are carnivores. **A carnivore is an organism that feeds mainly on meat.**
- The final consumer is called the top consumer.
- **A trophic level is a feeding stage in a food chain.**

The two food chains given above can be represented as follows:

Producer	Primary consumer	Secondary consumer	Tertiary consumer
1st trophic level	2nd trophic level	3rd trophic level	4th trophic level
Grass	Rabbit	Fox	
Dandelion	Snail	Thrush	Hawk

Length of food chains

A food chain is limited in length due to the huge loss of energy between each trophic level. Over 90% of the energy in each trophic level is not passed on to the next trophic level (much of it is lost as heat).

In the example of the grass → rabbit → fox food chain:

- The grass loses a great deal of energy in respiration
- Some grass leaves die and are not eaten by rabbits
- Less than 10% of the energy in the grass is passed on to the rabbits.

The same energy losses occur at each stage of the food chain. This means that the amount of energy available to the top consumer is relatively low.

Loss of energy in a food chain

Food web

A *food web* consists of two or more interlinked food chains.

A food web is an attempt to show the feeding relationships in an ecosystem in a more realistic way than in a food chain. The following is an example of a food web from a grassland ecosystem.

Point to note

A food web should have **two** producers and at least **nine** organisms.

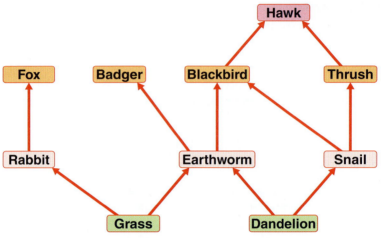

A food web from a grassland ecosystem

Pyramid of numbers

A *pyramid of numbers* represents the number of organisms at each stage (trophic level) in a food chain.

Pyramids of numbers are a way of comparing the number of organisms at different trophic levels in a food chain. The number of organisms at each trophic level in a food chain normally decreases. There are two reasons for this:

1   There is less energy at each trophic level.

2   The size of the organisms increases at each trophic level.

The pyramid of numbers for the food chain grass → rabbit → fox may be represented as follows:

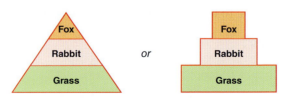

A pyramid of numbers

Limitations of the use of pyramids of numbers

1   Pyramids of numbers do not take into account the **size of organisms**. For example, if the producers are (millions of) grass plants, they form a wide base on the pyramid. However, if the producer is an oak tree or a rose bush that supports many greenfly, which in turn have many parasitic mites, then the base of the pyramid is very narrow, producing an inverted pyramid, as shown below.

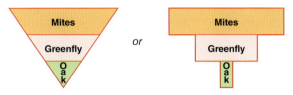

An inverted pyramid of numbers

2   Sometimes the number of organisms is so great that they cannot be represented properly on a pyramid of numbers. For example, hundreds of millions of bacteria or lice living on a dead badger cannot be drawn to scale.

Niche

A *niche* is the functional role of an organism in an ecosystem or habitat.
A niche often refers to what the organism eats. Each organism is adapted to occupy a different niche in the ecosystem. In general, no two organisms occupy the same niche (if they do, they will compete with each other). For example:

- Swallows and bats both eat insects. They occupy different food niches because swallows feed by day whereas bats feed by night.
- In a similar way, kestrels feed on animals such as mice by day and owls feed on mice at night.

Nutrient recycling

Nutrient recycling is the way in which elements or minerals are:

- Absorbed by organisms
- Released into the environment when the organisms decompose
- Absorbed by other organisms.

The carbon cycle

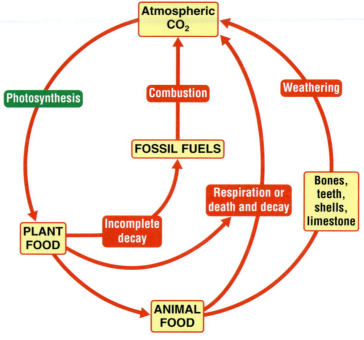

The carbon cycle

The organisms involved in the carbon cycle include the following:

- Plants and algae: remove CO_2 from the environment in photosynthesis and return it in respiration.
- Animals: obtain their carbon by eating plants and release carbon in respiration.
- Fungi and bacteria: return CO_2 to the environment when they decompose dead organisms.

Global warming

The concentration of carbon dioxide in the air is rising. The two main reasons for the rise in CO_2 are:

- Increased burning of fossil fuels such as coal and oil
- Destruction of the world's forests

Increased concentrations of CO_2 result in the planet becoming warmer, a process known as global warming.

The nitrogen cycle

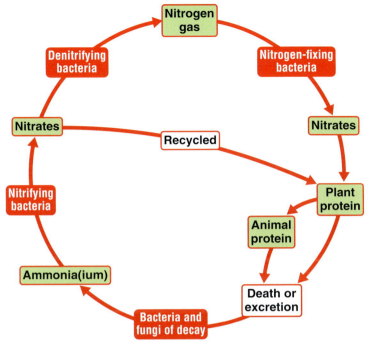

The nitrogen cycle

- Plants need nitrogen in order to make proteins. Plants cannot use nitrogen gas in the air (79%), as it is an inert gas.
- **Nitrogen-fixing bacteria** are found in swellings called nodules on the roots of a group of plants called legumes. Peas, beans and clover are legumes. Nitrogen-fixing bacteria convert nitrogen gas into nitrate. Plants can use nitrates to make proteins. They are symbiotic and are in fact mutualistic (as both the bacteria and the legumes benefit from the relationship).
- The nitrogen in plants is transferred to animals when they eat and assimilate plant proteins.
- When plants and animals die they are decomposed by **bacteria and fungi of decay** in the soil. Nitrogen compounds such as ammonium salts are released into the soil.
- **Nitrifying bacteria** in the soil convert ammonium salts into nitrites and then into nitrates.
- These nitrates may be absorbed by the roots of plants and recycled to make plant proteins.
- **Denitrifying bacteria** in the soil convert nitrates into nitrogen gas.

Organisms in the nitrogen cycle

Organism	Role
Nitrogen-fixing bacteria	Convert nitrogen gas to nitrates
Bacteria and fungi of decay	Convert proteins into nitrogen compounds such as ammonium salts
Nitrifying bacteria	Convert nitrogen compounds into nitrites and nitrates
Denitrifying bacteria	Convert nitrates into nitrogen gas

Population control

A *population* comprises all the members of a species in an area. All the rabbits in a field make up a population of rabbits. All the dandelions in a field make up a population of dandelions. A number of factors combine to control population numbers. These factors include competition, predation, parasitism and symbiosis.

Competition

***Competition* occurs when two or more organisms actively struggle for a resource that is in short supply.**

- Animals compete for factors such as food, water, shelter, territory and reproductive partners.
- Plants compete for space, light, water and minerals. Competition may occur between members of different species (**inter-specific competition**) and **always** occurs between members of the same species (**intra-specific competition**).

Types of competition

- ***Contest competition* occurs when one organism gets most (or all) of a resource and the other organism gets very little (or none) of the resource.** Contest competition means that there is a winner and a loser. An example of contest competition is when male deer compete with each other for mating rights with female deer. Birds, such as robins, also show contest competition when they defend their territories by singing.
- ***Scramble competition* means that all of the competing organisms get some of the resource.** An example of scramble competition is when seedlings grow in overcrowded conditions. All of the seedlings strive to get enough light, water, minerals and space but very often none of them can get enough of these resources.

Adaptations to survive competition

An *adaptation* is any alteration that improves an organism's chances of survival. In order to survive competition, organisms are adapted to their environment. For example:

- Dandelion leaves are adapted to grow close to the ground to prevent them from being eaten (or cut by mowers)
- Rabbits have good hearing, which helps them to avoid predators.

Predation

***Predation* is the catching, killing and eating of another organism for food.** The predator is the animal that catches, kills and eats; the prey is the animal killed and eaten.

Examples of predator–prey relationships include those between foxes and rabbits or hawks and mice.

Adaptations of predators

- The colour of a fox's coat helps to camouflage it.
- Hawks' excellent eyesight helps them to see their prey.

Adaptations of prey

- Rabbits have large hind legs, so they can run very fast.
- Mice are very flexible, which allows them to hide in very small spaces.

Parasitism

A *parasite* is a living thing that takes its food from another living thing (called a host) and usually causes harm.

Examples of parasites include fleas and mosquitoes on humans; tapeworms in humans; aphids (greenflies) and potato-blight fungus on plants; and liver fluke in cattle.

Symbiosis

***Symbiosis* occurs when two organisms from different species live, and have to live, in close association, where at least one of them benefits.**

- Parasitism is a form of symbiosis in which one species gains and the second species loses.
- **Mutualism** is another form of symbiosis, in which both organisms benefit.

An example of mutualism is nitrogen-fixing bacteria living in nodules of a plant such as clover.

The bacteria supply nitrates to the plant, while the plant provides food and shelter to the bacteria. Both species benefit from the relationship.

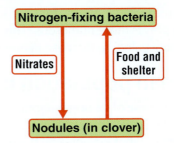

An example of symbiosis or mutualism

Population dynamics

Population dynamics refers to the factors that cause population numbers to rise or fall.

- Population numbers rise due to births or immigration (organisms moving into an area).
- Population numbers fall due to death or emigration (organisms moving out of an area).

Predator–prey relationships

The number of predators and prey are inter-related. This may result in a cyclic pattern of population dynamics, as shown by the graph.

Predator–prey relationships

The following variables or factors contribute to the changes in the number of predator and prey.

Availability of food

- When the predators first feed on the prey the predator numbers rise and the number of prey falls.
- The lower number of prey results in a fall in the predator numbers due to a lack of food.
- As the predator numbers fall the number of prey can rise again and the cycle resumes.

> **Remember**
>
> The predator numbers:
> Are lower than the prey numbers
> Reach a peak after the prey numbers.

Concealment

The prey are not completely wiped out because some of them may hide or conceal themselves from the predators. The small number of prey may reproduce and eventually increase in numbers.

Movement to new locations

When the number of prey falls too low the predators often move to a new location where prey is more numerous. This allows small groups of prey (which may have been concealed) to increase in number again in the old location.

Human population numbers

From the time of its origin about 200,000 years ago, the human population grew slowly. However, from the mid-1700s the number of humans has increased rapidly to produce what we now call the population explosion, as shown on the following graph.

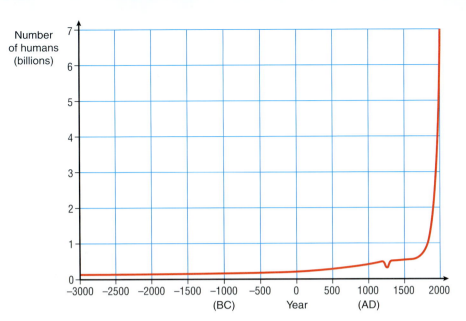

Human population numbers

Factors affecting human population numbers

- **War** reduces the number of humans. For example, in the Second World War twenty-two million people died. However, the reduction in numbers may be temporary due to the increased birth rate after a war finishes (the so-called baby boom).
- **Famine** reduces population numbers. Shortage of food leads to malnutrition and death due to disease. This was seen in the Great Irish Famine of 1845–1847 when about one million people died of starvation and disease.
- **Contraception** or birth control is the prevention of fertilisation. This reduces population numbers. In Ireland contraception (along with education and changes in society) has reduced the number of births per woman from over eight in the 1800s to 2.01 in 2013.
- **Disease** reduces the numbers in a population. This can be seen by the fall in human numbers shown on the graph in the fourteenth century due to bubonic plague (the Black Death). However, in the last one hundred years we have learned to cure or control many diseases. This has resulted in a huge increase in human population numbers.

Advances in disease control include:

- — Vaccination (against typhoid, cholera, TB, smallpox, etc.)
- — Improved sanitation (i.e. washing, disinfectants, food hygiene)
- — Insecticides (kill insects that spread diseases such as malaria, yellow fever and sleeping sickness)
- — Improved surgical methods (sterile equipment reduces wound infections)
- — Drugs such as antibiotics (have reduced bacterial infections).

Control and cure of disease has resulted in a huge rise in human numbers.

At present there are over seven billion people on Earth.

5 Human Impact on an Ecosystem

Learning objectives

In this chapter you will learn about:

1 Pollution
2 Conservation
3 Waste management

Pollution

Pollution is any harmful addition to the environment.

- Pollution results from unwanted materials called pollutants.
- Most pollution results from human sources such as litter, dumping, sewage disposal, noise and radioactivity.
- Natural sources of pollution include volcanoes and smoke from fires.
- Pollution may affect the air, fresh water, sea and land.

The effect of one pollutant

Pollutants, such as excessive fertiliser, animal waste or slurry (which acts as fertiliser), spread on grassland can have serious results.

> **Top Tip!**
> You are required to know the effects of **one** domestic, agricultural or industrial pollutant.

Excessive fertiliser

- If too much fertiliser is spread on grassland, the fertiliser may get washed into streams, rivers and lakes.
- The minerals in the fertiliser cause algae to grow in the water.
- When the algae die they are decomposed by bacteria. This uses up oxygen.
- All the oxygen in the water gets used up so that all living things die.
- This process is called eutrophication.

Control of pollution

- The use of fertiliser should be limited so that excess is not washed away.
- Animal waste, called slurry, should be spread on grassland only when grass is actively growing in spring and when the weather is dry.

Conservation

Conservation is the wise management of our existing natural resources in order to allow as many species as possible to survive (i.e. to maintain biodiversity).

Conservation is important in preventing the extinction of organisms such as red deer, red squirrels and rare orchids. In order to live as we do, humans alter the environment in many ways. For example:

- We destroy fields, hedges and woods in order to build houses, roads and factories.
- To grow crops and support animals we destroy natural habitats and sow single species of cereals or grass.
- We use weedkillers and insecticides along with artificial levels of fertiliser.
- To provide fuel we destroy woods and bogs and drill for oil and gas.

Top Tip!
You need to know of any **one** practice of conservation from the areas of agriculture, fisheries or forestry.

Example of conservation in agriculture

- The use of fertiliser and slurry should be controlled in order to prevent eutrophication in streams, rivers and lakes.
- Hedges should not be cut between March and August when birds are rearing their young.

Waste management

Top Tip!
You are required to know **one** example of waste management in the areas of agriculture, fisheries or forestry.

Wastes are produced in all homes, premises and industries. At present most waste is taken to landfill sites where it is dumped. Micro-organisms such as bacteria and fungi decompose the waste. However, there are too few landfill sites available to take the huge amount of waste that we are now producing. New strategies for managing waste need to be developed.

Example of waste management in agriculture

Animal waste, in the form of slurry, is stored in concrete pits. It is spread on the land in dry weather in spring to allow the minerals to be absorbed by plants (mainly grass). In this way the waste is recycled.

Problems with waste disposal

- Waste may contain disease-causing micro-organisms.
- Toxic chemicals from waste may leak into drinking-water supplies.
- Nutrients released from waste may cause eutrophication.
- Waste in landfill sites may be smelly and unsightly. It may also attract rats and gulls.
- Dumping at sea causes pollution of the oceans and may affect beaches and shorelines.
- Incinerators burn huge volumes of waste very rapidly at high temperatures. However, there are fears that harmful gases are released in the process.

Waste minimisation

The following steps (the three 'R's) should be taken in order to minimise the problems of waste disposal.

- **Reduce** the amount of unnecessary packaging that we use.
- **Re-use** as many items as possible. For example, the re-use of shopping bags has resulted in fewer waste plastic bags. Glass bottles and old clothes can also be re-used.
- **Recycle** as many materials as possible.
  — For example, paper, glass, aluminium and other metals, some plastics, and organic waste can all be recycled.
  — Almost half of all household waste is organic and may be broken down by bacteria to form compost. This material may be added to the soil to improve the growth of plants.
  — Spreading slurry on grassland allows minerals to be recycled.

Study of an Ecosystem

6

Study of a habitat

Studying a grassland

An ecosystem is too large to study. Instead we select smaller areas in the ecosystem to study. The local areas of study are called habitats. By studying a number of habitats we hope to gain an insight into the entire ecosystem.

Studying an ecosystem or habitat involves the following five steps:

1 Draw a sketch map of the area.

2 Identify the flora and fauna that are present.

3 Estimate the numbers of flora and fauna present.

4 Measure the abiotic factors.

5 Present the information you gathered.

Top Tip!

You are required to study any **one** ecosystem.

Within the selected ecosystem you are required to study ten organisms to include **five** flora (plants or algae) and **five** fauna (animals). You are required to have a detailed knowledge of only **one** flora or fauna.

Map of habitat

A rough sketch map of the habitat should be drawn. The map should show any special features, such as rocks, trees, streams or waterlogged areas. The map does not have to be too detailed.

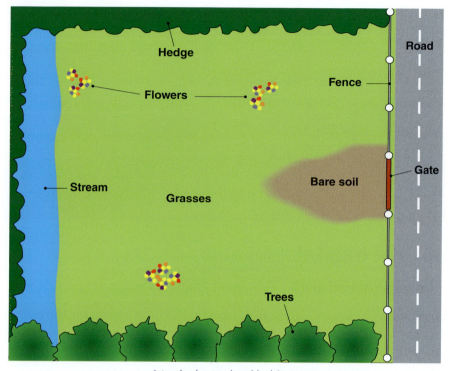

A typical grassland habitat

 ## Experiment

To collect flora and fauna

Direct search

Stationary organisms can be collected directly by picking them up. This is used for plants, fungi and animals such as snails and slugs.

Collection apparatus

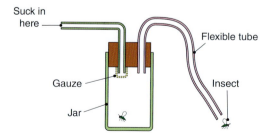

Pooter: used to collect insects and spiders

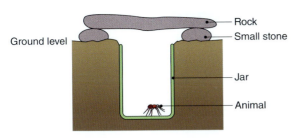

Ground level — Rock
— Small stone
— Jar
— Animal

Pitfall trap: used to collect insects, snails, woodlice, centipedes and millipedes

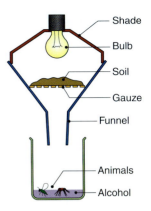

— Shade
— Bulb
— Soil
— Gauze
— Funnel
— Animals
— Alcohol

Tullgren funnel: used to separate small organisms from a soil sample. The heat of the bulb forces the animals out of the soil

Experiment

The use of simple keys to identify any five flora and any five fauna

Suitable keys for grassland plants, fungi and animals are used to identify the different organisms in the habitat. Where possible, organisms should be identified in their habitat, rather than elsewhere.

The key shown below can be used to identify the organisms A, B, C, D and E shown.

(The correct answers are given at the end of this chapter).

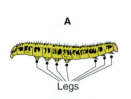

A

Legs

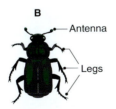

B

— Antenna

— Legs

C

D

E

1   Animal has a shell . . . .*Helix*
    Animal does not have a shell. . . . . Go to 2

2   Animal has legs. . . . . Go to 3
    Animal does not have legs . . . . Go to 4

3   Animal has three pairs of legs. . . . . *Tribolium*
    Animal has more than three pairs of legs. . . . . *Pieris* larva

4   Animal has long rounded body. . . . . Nematode
    Animal has flat body with two eye spots . . . . Planarian

A quantitative study of grassland

Study of a habitat

A *qualitative* study simply records whether something is present or absent.

A *quantitative* study records the numbers of each item.

Experiment

Using a quadrat to conduct a quantitative study of the plants in a habitat

1   A quadrat is a square frame made of metal, wood or plastic. Quadrats are made in different sizes, but the most commonly used are 0.5m x 0.5m (giving an area of 0.25 m²).

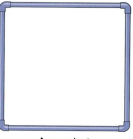

A quadrat

A grid quadrat

Sometimes the quadrat has gridlines. An organism is counted if it touches the intersection of two gridlines.

2   The quadrat is placed at random in the habitat. This is often carried out by throwing an object (such as a pencil) over your shoulder and placing the quadrat where the object lands.

3   Within each quadrat the percentage cover and frequency of each organism is measured.

4   The percentage cover refers to the percentage of each quadrat covered by each species. It is recorded as shown in the following table.

Species	Quadrat number										Number of quadrats containing plant	Frequency
	1	2	3	4	5	6	7	8	9	10		
Grass	80	90	90	90	80	20	70	80	30	90	10	100%
Nettles	0	0	0	0	0	60	0	0	40	0	2	20%
Dandelion	10	0	0	10	10	0	0	0	20	0	4	40%
Buttercup	0	10	0	0	0	10	0	0	10	0	3	30%
Daisy	0	10	10	0	0	0	10	10	0	0	4	40%

5   The frequency is the chance of a particular species being present in any quadrat.

It is calculated by counting the number of quadrats containing the particular species and dividing it by the total number of quadrats. For example, in the table shown nettles were found in two out of the ten quadrats. The frequency for nettles is: 2/10 × 100 = 20%.

Experiment

To conduct a quantitative study of the animals in a habitat using the capture/recapture method

1 This process involves capturing a number of animals (say snails) and marking them.

2 They are marked in a way that does not harm them or make them more obvious to predators (e.g. a small blob of paint is placed on the edge of the snail's shell, birds are ringed, and deer are tagged).

3 The animals are released close to where they were captured.

4 A few days later another sample of the animals is recaptured.

5 The number of marked animals in this sample is counted.

6 The number of animals in the population is estimated as follows:

$$\frac{\text{Number caught first time} \times \text{Number caught second time}}{\text{Number marked second time}}$$

7 For example, 40 snails are caught, marked and released. At a later date 40 more snails are caught and 25 of these are found to be marked. The total number of snails in the population is estimated as:

$$\frac{\text{Number caught first time} \times \text{Number caught second time}}{\text{Number marked second time}} = \frac{40 \times 40}{25} = 64$$

Measuring abiotic factors

Abiotic factors are non-living factors. They include factors such as soil pH, temperature, water content, humus content, mineral content, air temperature, light intensity, slope, exposure and water or air currents.

Top Tip!

You are required to measure any **three** abiotic factors.

Experiment

To measure three abiotic factors in a habitat

The following factors are measured at each station (or quadrat) in the habitat or along the belt transect.

1 The air temperature is recorded using a thermometer.

2 The light intensity is measured using a light meter.

3 The soil pH is measured using a pH meter or by using universal indicator.

Influence of abiotic factors

1 Fewer plants are found at low light intensities (e.g. in the shade of a hedge or tree).

2 There is less grass growing in areas where the soil water content is too high.

3 Nettles are found in soil with a high mineral content.

Adaption of an organism

Adaptations allow an organism to survive in its habitat. Adaptations may be structural or behavioural.

- **Structural**: Snails are covered by a shell for protection and to prevent them from drying out. Buttercups have creeping horizontal stems (called runners) to allow them to spread rapidly.
- **Behavioural**: Rabbits thump the ground with their back legs to signal danger. Daisy and dandelion flowers open in bright light to attract insects for pollination.

Sources of error in studying an ecosystem

- **Human error**: It is easy to take incorrect readings and measurements, especially if the weather is poor and the grassland is wet and uneven.
- **Changing conditions**: The organisms in an ecosystem may differ according to the seasons, the presence or absence of humans, weather conditions and whether it is day or night. All of these changing conditions alter the organisms identified and studied.
- **Accidental discoveries**: If an organism is very rare, it may be discovered only by accident. Similarly, if an organism (such as a fox or a bird of prey) is scared away by humans, it may be recorded in the ecosystem only if you come across it by chance. By studying a large number of habitats the chance of accidental discovery is reduced.
- **Sample size**: The more habitats that are examined in each ecosystem the more accurately the results will reflect the ecosystem. It is also important to use the correct size of quadrat or the results of the study will be invalid. For example, a small quadrat used in a study of a woodland will not show the presence of any trees.

Presenting the results of an ecosystem study

The results of your investigations should be presented in a report or portfolio of work. The portfolio should include most of the following:

- A note of any safety factors or precautions
- A diagram of the habitat
- Diagrams and details of any five plants and five animals
- A more detailed report on any one organism
- Details of how the organisms were collected
- Sample food chain, food web and pyramid of numbers from the ecosystem
- Details and results of the quantitative study in the form of tables, checklists, pie charts, histograms or graphs, as appropriate
- Examples of adaptation, competition, predation, parasitism and mutualism, where possible
- A list of any possible sources of error
- A note of any local factors that might affect the chosen habitat which should have been identified.

Answers

Answers for the key shown on p.29.

A *Pieris* larva

B *Tribolium*

C Planarian

D Nematode

E *Helix*

7 Cell Structure

Learning objectives

In this chapter you will learn about:

1 The light microscope
2 Plant and animal cells
3 Cell ultrastructure
4 Prokaryotic and eukaryotic cells

The light microscope

Part	Function
Eyepiece lens	Enlarges or magnifies the image
Nosepiece	Revolves to allow an objective lens to be used
Objective lens	Enlarges or magnifies the image
Focus knobs	Allow a clear image to be seen
Stage	Holds the microscope slide in place with clips
Diaphragm	Adjusts the amount of light passing through the slide
Mirror	Reflects a light source that passes through the slide (it may be replaced by a direct light source)

The total magnification is found by multiplying the powers of the two lenses. For example, if the eyepiece is marked x10 and the objective lens is marked x20, the total magnification is x200.

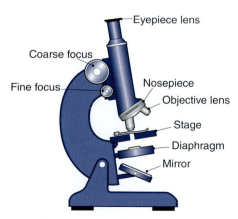

The parts of a light microscope

Experiment

To use a light microscope

1 Move the stage down as low as possible.

2 Place a prepared slide on the stage.

3 Move the slide so that the material you wish to see is in the centre of the stage.

4 Place the clips on the slide.

5 Move the stage up as close to the objective lens as possible.

6 Rotate the nosepiece so that the low-power lens is in place. Looking through the eyepiece, slowly move the coarse focus knob so that the objective lens rises.

7 Use the coarse focus knob to adjust the low-power lens upwards so that the image is in focus.

8 When a clear image is seen, adjust the light using the diaphragm or a sheet of paper.

9 Gently reposition the slide so that what you want to see is in the centre.

10 Rotate the nosepiece so that the high-power objective lens is in place.

11 Use the fine focus knob to produce a clear image.

Experiment

To examine plant and animal cells under a microscope

To examine plant cells under a microscope

1 Use a forceps to remove a thin strip of cells from a cut-up onion.

2 Place the onion cells on a microscope slide.

3 Add a few drops of stain (such as iodine).

4 Add a cover slip at an angle *(to eliminate air bubbles)*.

5 Blot off any excess stain if necessary.

6 Examine the cells under low power and then under high power, as outlined in the previous experiment.

7 The cells appear as shown.

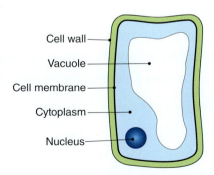

Plant cell as seen under light microscope

To examine animal cells under a microscope

1   Scrape the inside of your mouth with a lollipop stick or a cotton wool bud.

2   Rub the stick or bud on a microscope slide.

3   Add a few drops of stain (such as methylene blue).

4   Add a cover slip at an angle *(to eliminate air bubbles)*.

5   Blot off any excess stain if necessary.

6   Examine the cells under low power and then under high power.

7   The cells appear as shown.

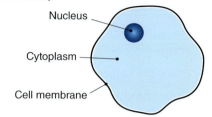

Animal cell as seen under light microscope

Plant and animal cells

Plant cells

- Plant cells are surrounded by a cell wall made of cellulose. The cell wall gives strength to a plant cell. Inside the cell wall is a cell membrane.
- Many plant cells have a large vacuole. The vacuole contains a liquid called cell sap. The vacuole gives strength to the cell by pushing out against the cell wall (in the same way that the air in a car tyre helps to support the car).

Animal cells

- Animal cells have no cell wall; they are surrounded by a cell or plasma membrane.
- Animal cells do not have vacuoles.

Cell ultrastructure

***Ultrastructure* refers to the appearance of structures as seen under an electron microscope.**

Electron microscopes magnify and produce sharp images of an object much better than a light microscope.

- A transmission electron microscope shows the internal structure of an object.
- A scanning electron microscope shows a surface view of an object.

Biological membranes

All the membranes in and around a cell have the same structure. They are made of a double layer of phospholipid. Proteins are embedded in the phospholipid bilayer.

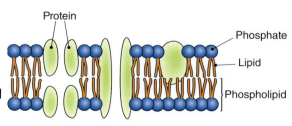

Ultrastructure of a membrane

The functions of membranes include:

- Retention of liquid contents
- Recognition of molecules
- Control of what passes in and out through the membrane

Nucleus

The nucleus contains a specific number of chromosomes. Chromosomes are made of DNA and protein. They are normally elongated and appear as chromatin.

The function of the nucleus is to control the cell.

Nucleolus

One or more nucleoli are often seen as dark circles in the nucleus. They make ribosomes (which are composed of RNA).

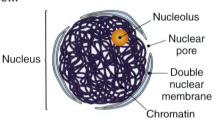

The nucleus and nucleolus

Cytoplasm

The cytoplasm is the area in the cell surrounding the nucleus. It contains many cell organelles (such as mitochondria and ribosomes). If the cell organelles are removed from the cytoplasm, the remaining liquid is called the cytosol. **The cytosol is the liquid part of the cytoplasm.**

Mitochondrion

A double membrane surrounds each mitochondrion (with the inner membrane showing many infoldings, as seen in the diagram). Respiration takes place in the mitochondria. This means that mitochondria supply energy to the cell.

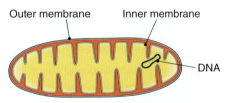

The structure of a mitochondrion

- Active cells (e.g. muscle in animals and growth or meristematic cells in plants) have many mitochondria.
- Inactive cells (e.g. fat in animals and ground tissue in plants) have few mitochondria.

Ribosomes

Ribosomes are tiny round structures. They are made of RNA and protein. Their function is to make protein.

Chloroplasts

Chloroplasts are green and surrounded by a double membrane. Photosynthesis takes place in chloroplasts.

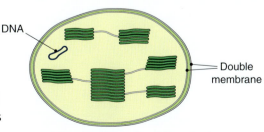

The structure of a chloroplast

The differences between plant and animal cells

Plant cell	Animal cell
Has cell wall	No cell wall
Has chloroplasts	No chloroplasts
Has chlorophyll	No chlorophyll
Has a large vacuole	No vacuole

Prokaryotic and eukaryotic cells

***Prokaryotic* cells do not have a nucleus or cell structures that are enclosed by membranes**

In addition prokaryotic cells:

- Are usually small
- Do not have mitochondria or chloroplasts
- Are primitive
- Include bacteria, which are in the kingdom Monera.

> **Point to note**
>
> 'Pro' means first and prokaryotic cells were the first cells to evolve.

***Eukaryotic cells* have a membrane enclosed nucleus and cell organelles**

In addition eukaryotic cells:

- Are larger than prokaryotic cells
- Contain structures such as mitochondria and chloroplasts that are enclosed by membranes
- Are more advanced than prokaryotic cells
- Include plant and animal cells along with cells from the kingdoms Protoctista (protists) and Fungi.

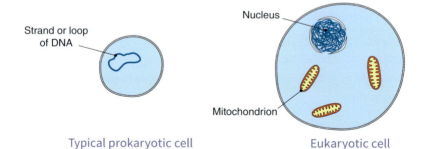

Typical prokaryotic cell   Eukaryotic cell

Cell Diversity

8

Learning objectives

In this chapter you will learn about:

1 Tissues
2 Plant tissues
3 Animal tissues
4 Tissue culture
5 Organs
6 Organ systems

Tissues

A *tissue* is a group of similar cells that carry out the same function(s).

Top Tip!

You are required to study only **two** plant and **two** animal tissues.

Plant tissues

Plant tissues include dermal, vascular and ground tissues.

Dermal tissue

Dermal tissue surrounds and encloses plants. The epidermis is an example of a dermal tissue.

- **Location:** dermal tissue is found (as epidermis) in the leaf, stem and roots.
- **Appearance:** epidermal tissue usually contains rectangular cells. The cells normally have thick, strong walls. They often have a waterproof layer (the cuticle) on their outer surface.

Cuticle
Cell wall

Function

The main function of dermal tissue is to protect. If a cuticle is present, the secondary function is to prevent water loss.

Vascular tissue

The word 'vascular' means 'transport'. There are two types of vascular tissue in plants: xylem and phloem.

Location: xylem and phloem are found in all parts of the plant, i.e. in the roots, stems and leaves. They are usually arranged in bundles called vascular bundles.

Xylem

There are two types of xylem tissue: tracheids and vessels. Both of these tissues are dead at maturity, i.e. the cells do not have a nucleus and cytoplasm.

Tracheids

- Appearance: tracheids are long narrow tubes formed when the sloping walls of individual cells overlap. Their walls have small openings called pits that allow water to pass from cell to cell.
- Lignin is a strong material found around all types of xylem. It helps to strengthen both the xylem and the plant.
- Tracheids are more primitive and less efficient than vessels.

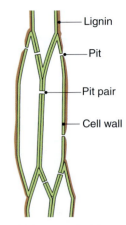

Xylem tracheids

Vessels

- Appearance: vessels are larger than tracheids. The end walls of the cells break down in vessels to form a continuous hollow tube.
- Vessels have lignin and are very common in flowering plants and in trees, where they form the wood.

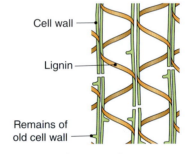

Xylem vessel

Function

The main function of both tracheids and vessels is to transport water.

A second function of xylem is to give strength to the plant (due to lignin).

Phloem

Phloem cells are alive at maturity. For this reason phloem is called a living tissue. There is only one type of phloem.

- Appearance: phloem consists of many cells that join together to form long tubes called sieve tubes.
- The walls at the end of each phloem cell have many pores so that they look like sieves. This is why they are called sieve plates.
- The sieve tubes do not have nuclei, but each accompanying companion cell contains a nucleus. The companion cells control the activity of the associated phloem element.

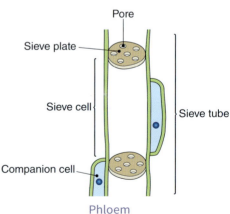

Phloem

Function

Phloem transports food from the photosynthetic regions to the rest of the plant. The companion cells control the phloem cells.

Animal tissues

Animal tissues include epithelial, connective, muscular and nervous tissues.

Connective tissue

Connective tissue joins and supports other parts of the body. It consists of cells contained in a matrix (a surrounding substance). Examples include adipose tissue (fat under the skin), cartilage, bone and blood.

Top Tip!
You must know about **two** of these four tissues.

Blood is a connective tissue as it has red cells (to carry oxygen), white cells (to fight infection) and platelets (to clot the blood) suspended in a matrix called plasma.

Nervous tissue

Nervous tissue consists of nerve cells called neurons. These cells are adapted to carry electrical impulses to and from the brain, as outlined in Chapter 31.

Tissue culture

***Tissue culture* is the growth of cells on an artificial medium outside an organism.**

- The growth of cells **outside** the body is called in-vitro (from *vitreus* meaning 'glass').
- The growth of cells **in** the body is called in-vivo (from *vivus* meaning 'living').

In-vitro growth requires the following conditions:

- The correct nutrients (e.g. carbohydrates, amino acids, vitamins, minerals)
- Growth hormones
- A suitable temperature
- A suitable pH
- Oxygen (usually required)
- A sterile environment (this means there are no bacteria or fungi, which grow too fast and produce toxic waste products).

Examples of tissue culture:

Micropropagation is the growth of large numbers of identical plants from pieces of an original plant. In micro-propagation a suitable plant is selected. It is cut into small pieces consisting of one or a few cells. These pieces are grown artificially to produce new plants that are genetically identical to the

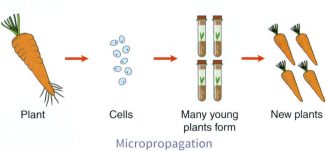

Plant   Cells   Many young plants form   New plants

Micropropagation

original plant. These plants can then be transplanted into soil and grown as normal.

Benefits of micropropagation:

- — A huge number of plants can be produced in a very short time
- — The new plants are genetically identical
- — The process is a cheap way to produce new plants.

Cancer research can be carried out on cells that are grown artificially outside the body in containers. In this way the effect of new drugs and treatments can be tested on cells without harming individual patients.

Skin grafts can now be carried out using cells taken from the patient that are grown in containers.

Organs

An *organ* is a structure composed of two or more tissues that work together to carry out one or more functions.

Plant organs include roots, stems, leaves and flowers.

The leaf is an organ that contains dermal tissue (upper and lower epidermis) for protection and vascular tissue (vascular bundles of xylem and phloem) for transport.

Animal organs include the brain, heart, lungs and kidneys.

The heart is an organ that contains the four types of animal tissue.

- The walls of the heart are made of cardiac muscle that pumps the blood.
- The pericardium (epithelial tissue) is the membrane around the heart.
- Blood and blood vessels are connective tissue.
- Heartbeat is controlled by the pacemaker, a type of nervous tissue.

Organ systems

An *organ system* consists of a group of organs working together to carry out one or more functions.

Examples of organ systems

There are ten organ systems in humans. All of these are essential for the individual to stay alive (except for the reproductive system).

The **digestive system** consists of the mouth, oesophagus, stomach, small and large intestines. All of these parts work together to take in, break down and absorb food.

The **circulatory system** consists of the heart, blood, blood vessels, lymph and lymph vessels. All of these parts work together to transport materials around the body.

> **Remember**
> cells → tissues → organs → organ systems

Enzymes 9

Learning objectives

In this chapter you will learn about:

1 Enzymes
2 Factors affecting enzyme action
3 Immobilised enzymes

Enzymes

An *enzyme* is a protein that speeds up a reaction without being used up in the reaction.

Enzymes can also be described as biological or organic catalysts. They control metabolism.

***Metabolism* is the sum of all the chemical reactions taking place in an organism.** Metabolism includes catabolism and anabolism.

Energy sources for reactions

- The Sun (solar energy) is the original source of all the energy on Earth.
  In photosynthesis **solar energy** is converted into the chemical energy in the bonds of biomolecules such as glucose.
- The energy in chemical bonds is called **cellular energy**. This energy is released in respiration and is used by living things to allow metabolism.

Features of enzyme action

- **The *substrate* is the molecule that an enzyme acts on.**
- **The *products* are the molecules produced by enzyme action.**
- Enzymes work because they have the correct shape to attach to the substrate.
- **The *active site* is that part of the enzyme that joins to the substrate.**

- The **induced fit theory** of enzyme action says that the active site has the approximate shape of the substrate. The active site changes shape slightly (when the substrate joins with the enzyme) to make an exact fit. Once the reaction is complete the active site returns to its original shape.

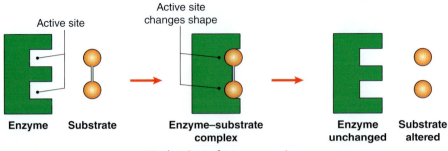

Mechanism of enzyme action

- ***Specificity* means that each enzyme can only join with one substrate.**
- Enzyme reactions are **reversible**. This means that the same enzyme can join two molecules to form a larger one (anabolic) or it can break down the larger molecule to form two simpler ones (catabolic).

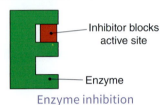

Enzyme inhibition

- **Inhibitors** are molecules that prevent an enzyme from working. They do this by blocking the active site of the enzyme.

Factors affecting enzyme action

The rate at which an enzyme works is affected by factors such as temperature and pH.

Temperature

- At 0°C water freezes to ice. This means that enzymes and substrate molecules cannot move. For this reason the rate of enzyme action is zero at 0°C.

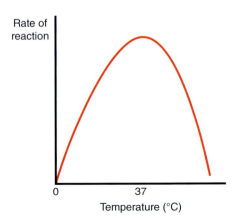

- As the temperature rises, molecules move faster. This causes enzymes and substrate molecules to collide more often. For this reason the rate of enzyme reaction increases with temperature.
- Above a certain temperature the shape of an enzyme begins to change.

This temperature is 37°C for human enzymes. Above this temperature the rate of reaction begins to fall.

- At higher temperatures the shape of the active site is changed permanently. The enzyme loses its ability to work and is said to be denatured.
- **A *denatured enzyme* has lost its shape and its ability to function.**

pH

- The pH scale runs from 0 to 14 (0–7 is acidic, 7 is neutral, 7–14 is basic or alkaline).
- Most enzymes work best at a pH close to 7 (pH 7 is the optimum pH for most enzymes).

The *optimum* pH is the pH at which the enzyme works best.

- At lower or higher pH values the shape of the active site becomes altered. This reduces the rate of the enzyme reaction.
- Enzymes can be denatured by unsuitable pH values.
- Note that pepsin is an enzyme that is adapted to work in the stomach at a pH of 2 and catalase works best at pH 9.

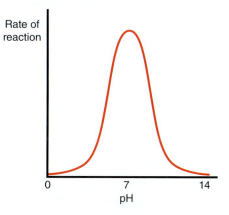

To investigate the effect of pH on the rate of enzyme action

Catalase is an enzyme found in a wide variety of living things such as liver, celery and potatoes. Catalase converts a toxic substance called hydrogen peroxide (H_2O_2) into water and oxygen.

$$2H_2O_2 \rightarrow 2H_2O + O_2$$

In the following investigation the oxygen forms foam. The volume of foam indicates the activity of the enzyme, i.e. the more foam there is, the greater the activity of the enzyme.

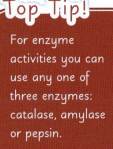

Top Tip!

For enzyme activities you can use any one of three enzymes: catalase, amylase or pepsin.

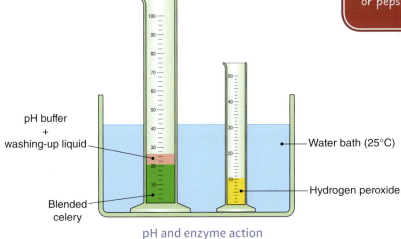

pH buffer + washing-up liquid

Blended celery

Water bath (25°C)

Hydrogen peroxide

pH and enzyme action

1   Put some pH buffer 4 into a graduated cylinder. *(This ensures that the pH will be 4.)*

2   Add one drop of washing-up liquid to the graduated cylinder. *(This will allow the oxygen to form foam.)*

3   Blend some celery in a blender with water. Filter the solution using coffee filter paper and add some of the filtrate to the graduated cylinder. *(The filtrate contains the enzyme catalase.)*

4   Add hydrogen peroxide to a smaller graduated cylinder. *(The hydrogen peroxide is the substrate.)*

5   Stand the graduated cylinders in a water bath at 25°C for a few minutes. *(This allows all the reagents to be at the same temperature.)*

6   Pour the hydrogen peroxide into the graduated cylinder and immediately note the combined volume of liquid in the graduated cylinder. *(This will be used to calculate the final volume of foam.)*

7   Record the volume at the top of the foam after 2 minutes.

8   Subtract the original volume of liquid in the cylinder from the final volume of foam. *(To calculate the volume of foam produced.)*

9   Repeat steps 1 to 8 using different pH buffers, e.g. pH buffers 7, 10 and 13.

The results can be shown as follows:

pH	4	7	10	13
Volume of foam (cm³)	0	65	128	0

10 As a **control**, use the same materials, but leave out the blended celery or use blended celery that has been boiled (i.e. leave out the enzyme or use denatured enzyme). In this case no foam should form.

Experiment

To investigate the effect of temperature on the rate of enzyme activity

1 Put some pH buffer 9 in a graduated cylinder. *(This ensures that the pH will be 9, which is the optimum pH for catalase.)*

2 Add one drop of washing-up liquid to the graduated cylinder. *(This will allow the oxygen to form visible foam.)*

3 Blend some celery in a blender with water. Filter the solution using coffee filter paper and add some of this filtrate to the graduated cylinder. *(The filtrate contains the enzyme catalase.)*

4 Add hydrogen peroxide to a smaller graduated cylinder. *(The hydrogen peroxide is the substrate.)*

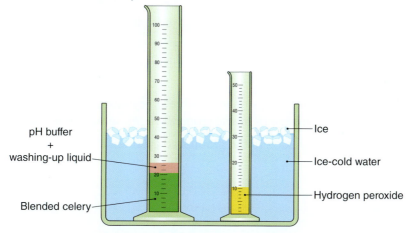

Temperature and enzyme action

5 Stand the graduated cylinders in a beaker of ice-cold water until they are at 0°C. *(This allows all the reagents to be at the same temperature.)*

6 Pour the hydrogen peroxide into the graduated cylinder and immediately note the combined volume of liquid in the graduated cylinder. *(This will be used to calculate the final volume of foam.)*

7 Record the volume at the top of the foam after 2 minutes.

8 Subtract the original volume of liquid added to the cylinder from the final volume of foam. *(To calculate the volume of foam produced.)*

9 Repeat steps 1 to 8, changing the temperature of the water bath in step 5 to 10°, 20°, 30°, 40°, 50° and 60°C.

The results can be shown as follows:

Temp. (°C)	0	10	20	30	40	50	60
Volume of foam (cm³)	0	23	97	99	54	21	8

10 As a **control**, use the same materials but leave out the blended celery or use blended celery that has been boiled (i.e. leave out the enzyme or use denatured enzyme). In this case no foam should form.

 Experiment

To investigate the denaturation of an enzyme by heat

1 Blend some celery in a blender with water. Filter the solution using coffee filter paper. *(The filtrate contains the enzyme catalase.)*

2 Boil half of the filtrate for 5 minutes or place it in a boiling water bath for 10 minutes. *(The high temperature denatures the enzyme.)*

3 Add some of the boiled filtrate to a graduated cylinder and place it in a water bath at 25°C.

4 Add pH buffer 9 and one drop of washing-up liquid to the same graduated cylinder.

5 Add hydrogen peroxide to a smaller graduated cylinder and place it in the same water bath. *(This brings all the reagents to the same temperature.)*

6 Add the hydrogen peroxide to the graduated cylinder.

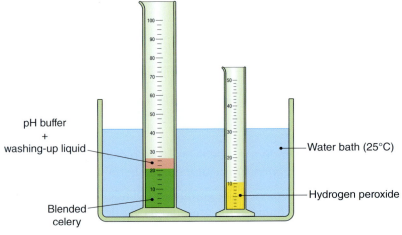

Heat denaturation of an enzyme

7 Record the original volume of liquid and the final volume after 2 minutes.

8 Calculate the volume of foam produced. *(This indicates the activity of the enzyme, if any.)*

9 Repeat the process using unboiled celery or catalase.

The results can be shown as follows:

	Volume of foam (cm^3)
Boiled enzyme	0
Unboiled enzyme	99

10 The conclusion is that boiling catalase prevents it from breaking down hydrogen peroxide.

Immobilised enzymes

Bioprocessing is the use of enzyme-controlled reactions to make a product. Traditional forms of bioprocessing involve the use of enzymes in organisms such as yeast and bacteria to produce substances such as cheese, yoghurt, bread, beer, wine and antibiotics.

More recently, it has become possible to use isolated enzymes to carry out some of these reactions. However, isolated enzymes, such as those in washing powders, are lost each time they are used.

Immobilised enzymes are attached to each other or to an inert substance. Enzymes are immobilised by attaching them to each other or to a separate substance or enclosing them in a gel or membrane. The substrate for the reaction is passed over the immobilised enzymes to allow the reaction to take place. The product is collected, leaving the enzymes to be reused.

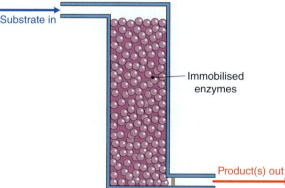

Benefits of immobilised enzymes

1 The enzymes, which are often very expensive, can be reused many times.

2 The product contains no enzyme (this saves on separation costs).

3 They are as efficient as (or sometimes more efficient than) isolated enzymes.

Examples of the uses of immobilised enzymes

1 Glucose is often used as a sweetener in foods, e.g. in soft drinks.

Fructose is a much sweeter but very expensive sugar. An immobilised enzyme called glucose isomerase is used to convert glucose to fructose.

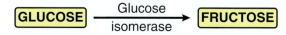

2   Penicillin is an antibiotic used to control bacterial growth. However, bacteria have evolved resistance to penicillin. A very expensive enzyme called penicillin acylase can be used to convert penicillin into more active antibiotics.

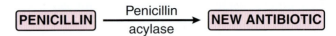

$$\boxed{\textbf{PENICILLIN}} \xrightarrow[\text{acylase}]{\text{Penicillin}} \boxed{\textbf{NEW ANTIBIOTIC}}$$

3   Enzymes can be immobilised on paper or plastic strips and used to detect (or diagnose) specific substances. For example, Clinistix contain an enzyme that changes colour when it reacts with a specific chemical. In this way they can be used to test for substances such as glucose or pregnancy hormones in urine.

Experiment

To prepare an enzyme immobilisation and examine its application

Yeast cells contain the enzyme sucrase, which converts sucrose to glucose. If yeast cells are immobilised, sucrase is immobilised.

1   Stir sodium alginate in a beaker of water until it is smooth. *(Sodium alginate forms the gel which will surround and immobilise the enzyme.)*

2   Mix yeast and water. *(Yeast contains the enzyme sucrase.)*

3   Add the yeast mixture to the alginate and stir.

4   Draw the yeast/alginate mixture into a syringe which does not have a needle attached. *(The needle would be too small an opening for the alginate beads to form.)*

5   Add calcium chloride to water in a beaker.

6   Slowly and steadily allow drops of the alginate/yeast mixture to fall into the calcium chloride solution, stirring the mixture as you add the drops.

7   Leave the beads in the calcium chloride for 15 minutes. *(This allows them to harden.)*

8   Place the beads in a sieve and wash them in a stream of tap water. *(This will remove non-immobilised yeast cells from outside the hardened beads.)*

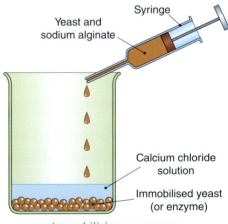

Immobilising an enzyme

9   The beads can be used immediately or they can be stored in water or dried in filter paper and stored in a fridge.

Application of immobilised enzyme

1   Place short straws in two separating funnels. *(The straws stop the beads of immobilised enzyme from blocking the outflow of liquid.)*

2   Mix yeast with water and place in a separating funnel. *(This free yeast acts as a control.)*

3   Place an equal volume of immobilised yeast cells in a second separating funnel.

4   Add equal volumes of the same sucrose solution to each of the separating funnels.

5   Adjust the taps so that the liquid drips slowly out of each separating funnel.

6   Use glucose test strips (such as Clinistix or Diastrix) to test for the presence of glucose coming out of each funnel.

7   Note the time taken in each funnel for glucose to be produced first.

8   Compare the cloudiness (or turbidity) of each of the beakers. *(The product from the free yeast will appear very cloudy; the product of the immobilised yeast will be clearer.)*

9   The results can be shown as follows.

	Free yeast or enzyme (control)	Immobilised yeast or enzyme
Time taken for glucose to form (minutes)	3	5
Cloudiness	Cloudy	Clear

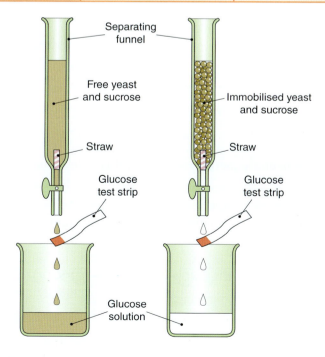

10 Photosynthesis

Learning objectives

In this chapter you will learn about:

1 Energy carriers
2 Introduction to photosynthesis
3 Location of photosynthesis
4 Sources of light, CO_2 and water for photosynthesis
5 Details of light and dark stages

Energy carriers

ATP

ATP is an energy-rich molecule. It is the molecule that is most often used by cells to supply energy for cell reactions.

NADPH

NADPH is an energy-rich molecule used to carry electrons and hydrogen ions in photosynthesis.

Top Tip!

NADPH has the letter **P** and is involved in **p**hotosynthesis.

NADH

NADH is an equivalent energy-rich molecule used to carry electrons and hydrogen in respiration. NADH will be dealt with in the chapter on respiration.

ADP and ATP

Adenosine diphosphate (better known as ADP) is a low-energy molecule.

ADP consists of a molecule called adenine that is attached to a carbohydrate called ribose. These two molecules form adenosine. Adenosine is attached to two phosphate molecules, as shown in the following diagram.

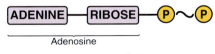

Structure of ADP

The bond between the two phosphates (shown as ~) is an unstable bond.

If energy is added to ADP in the form of another unstable phosphate ~ phosphate bond, **adenosine triphosphate (ATP)** is formed.

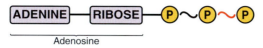

Structure of ATP

The formation of ATP in this way can be summarised as follows:

ADP + energy + P → ATP + water

ATP is the molecule that supplies the energy for most cell reactions. Active cells break down millions of ATP molecules every second:

ATP + water → ADP + P + energy

The bond between the last two phosphates in ATP contains the energy that is released to allow other cell reactions to proceed.

NADP and NADPH

$NADP^+$ is a low-energy molecule involved in photosynthesis. $NADP^+$ can combine with two high-energy electrons **(2e⁻)** and a single proton (also called a hydrogen ion or H^+) to form NADPH. This reaction can be shown as:

$NADP^+ + 2e^- + H^+$ → NADPH

When NADPH breaks down, it releases high-energy electrons and a hydrogen ion as shown below:

NADPH → $NADP^+ + 2e^- + H^+$

Introduction to photosynthesis

- Photosynthesis is a process by which light energy from the Sun is combined with carbon dioxide gas and water to form glucose and oxygen. A green pigment called chlorophyll is needed as a catalyst for this process.
- Photosynthesis is probably the most important process on Earth. It converts solar energy into chemical energy in the bonds of food biomolecules. The energy in food is then used to allow other biological reactions to take place.

SOLAR ENERGY ——Photosynthesis——→ CHEMICAL ENERGY

The balanced equation for photosynthesis is:

$$6CO_2 + 6H_2O \xrightarrow[\text{Chlorophyll}]{\text{Light}} C_6H_{12}O_6 + 6O_2$$

Role of photosynthesis

Photosynthesis is important because it:

- Makes food for plants
- Makes food for animals (when they eat plants)
- Forms oxygen for plants and animals
- Forms fossil fuels.

Location of photosynthesis

Photosynthesis depends on chlorophyll. In most cells chlorophyll is located in structures called chloroplasts. This means that photosynthesis takes place in chloroplasts.

Chloroplasts are heavily concentrated in cells (called palisade cells) in the upper surfaces of leaves. However, they are also present in the green stems of some plants.

Sources of light, CO_2 and water for photosynthesis

- Light normally comes from the Sun.
- Carbon dioxide comes from two sources:
  - Most CO_2 diffuses into the plant from the air. In leaves this happens through openings called stomata on the underside of the leaf.
  - Some CO_2 is produced within the plant by respiration.
- Water enters the roots of the plant from the soil. It passes up through xylem tubes to the leaves.

Promoting crop growth in greenhouses

The growth of crops in greenhouses can be promoted or increased in two ways.

1. Artificial light can be used to increase the intensity of the light and/or to increase the length of time the plant is exposed to light.

2. The air in the greenhouse can be enriched by adding carbon dioxide. This can be produced by burning gas or can be released from cylinders.

 Experiment

To investigate the influence of light intensity or carbon dioxide concentration on the rate of photosynthesis

1. Add sodium hydrogen carbonate (sodium bicarbonate) to water in a test tube until it will no longer dissolve. *(This ensures a constant concentration of carbon dioxide.)*

Top Tip!

There is a choice of experiment here. This chapter will deal with the influence of **light intensity** on the rate of photosynthesis.

2 Set up the apparatus as shown in the diagram. Note the distance of the lamp from the apparatus starts at 1 m. *(The Elodea carries out photosynthesis, the water bath ensures a constant temperature and the lamp provides light.)*

3 Leave the apparatus for a few minutes. *(This allows the plant to adjust its rate of photosynthesis to the new conditions.)*

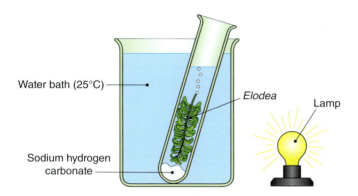

4 Count the number of bubbles emerging from the plant per minute. *(The number of bubbles indicates the rate of photosynthesis.)*

5 Repeat the previous step twice more and calculate the average number of bubbles per minute. *(This reduces the chance of unusual results.)*

6 Convert the number of bubbles per minute to light intensity using the formula $10\,000/\text{distance}^2$, where the distance is given in cm.

7 Move the lamp 20 cm closer to the apparatus. Allow the plant 2 minutes to adjust. *(Moving the lamp closer increases the light intensity.)*

8 Count the number of bubbles per minute over 3 minutes and calculate the average.

9 Repeat steps 7 and 8 until the lamp is 20 cm from the apparatus.

10 Record the results as follows.

Distance (cm)	Light intensity ($10\,000 / d^2$)	Number of bubbles / minute	Average number of bubbles / minute
100	1	6, 4, 5	5
80	1.56	12, 12, 12	12
60	2.8	22, 21, 20	21
40	6.25	27, 26, 28	27
20	25	31, 33, 32	32

11 Plot a graph of the results showing light intensity on the horizontal axis and rate of photosynthesis on the vertical axis. The graph should be similar to the one shown below.

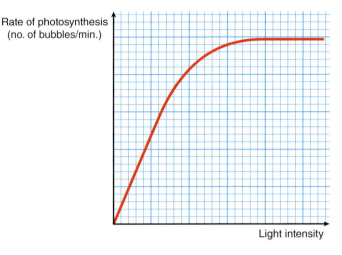

Rate of photosynthesis (no. of bubbles/min.)

Light intensity

12 The experiment and the graph show that increasing the light intensity increases the rate of photosynthesis, up to a point. Beyond a certain light intensity the rate of photosynthesis levels off.

13 As a **control**, the same apparatus can be set up in the dark. In this case no bubbles are produced.

Details of light and dark stages

- Photosynthesis occurs in two stages or phases: the light stage and the dark stage. Both of these stages take place in the chloroplast.
- **The *light stage* requires light and can take place only in the light.**
- **The *dark stage* does not require light and can take place in light or dark.** However, the dark stage uses molecules that are made in the light stage. This means that the dark stage requires the light stage to have taken place.

Top Tip!

The light stage uses light; the dark stage does not.

The light stage

1 Light is absorbed

All of the colours (except green) in white light are absorbed by chlorophyll and a variety of other pigments. These pigments are located in the chloroplast.

2 Light energy is transferred to electrons

Energy is passed through a cluster of pigments until it reaches a specially placed chlorophyll molecule. Electrons in this chlorophyll molecule become energised. The high-energy electrons pass from the chlorophyll to an electron acceptor. From the electron acceptor the electrons flow along either pathway 1 or pathway 2.

3 Electron flow

Pathway 1

In pathway 1 a single electron from chlorophyll flows along a sequence of electron acceptors. However, the electrons return or recycle back to the chlorophyll molecule. The electrons lose energy as they move along pathway 1. This energy is used to convert ADP into ATP as shown below.

ADP + energy + P → ATP + water

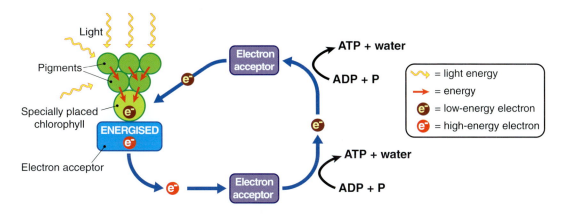

Pathway 2

In pathway 2 a pair of electrons leaves the specially placed chlorophyll and passes along a sequence of electron carriers.

At one point the pair of electrons joins with $NADP^+$ to form $NADP^-$, as shown below.

$NADP^+$ + 2 energised electrons → $NADP^-$

The chlorophyll molecule is now short of two electrons. It regains electrons supplied when water is split using light energy according to the equation:

$$2H_2O \xrightarrow{\text{Light}} 4H^+ + 4 \text{ electrons} + O_2$$

The hydrogen ions (H^+ or protons) formed when water is split are stored in the chloroplasts. When necessary, one of them combines with $NADP^-$ to form NADPH as shown below.

$NADP^-$ + H^+ → NADPH

As the electrons flow from acceptor to acceptor in pathway 2 they lose energy. Some of this energy is used to convert ADP to ATP as shown below.

ADP + energy + P → ATP + water

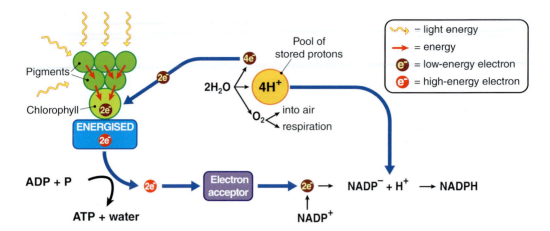

End products of the light stage:

There are three main end products formed in the light stage.

1   ATP is made in both pathways 1 and 2. This ATP will provide the energy for the events in the dark stage.

2   NADPH is made in pathway 2. This will supply protons and high-energy electrons for the events of the dark stage.

3   Oxygen is released when water is split in pathway 2.
    — Most of this oxygen passes out of the leaf into the air.
    — Some of the oxygen is used in respiration.

The dark stage

- The dark stage does not need light, but it does need NADPH and ATP made in the light stage.
- NADPH is used to supply hydrogen ions (H^+) and electrons while ATP supplies energy for the dark-stage reactions.
- While there are no enzymes used in the light stage, the dark-stage reactions are controlled by enzymes. This means that the rate of the dark stage is controlled by temperature.
- The dark stage also takes place in the chloroplast.

Events in the dark stage

- In the dark stage, hydrogen ions (H^+) released from NADPH combine with carbon dioxide to form glucose. The addition of hydrogen to a molecule is called reduction. Carbon dioxide is said to be reduced to form glucose.
- The energy to make glucose is supplied by the breakdown of ATP to form ADP and phosphate.

These events are summarised in the following equation:

ATP + water $\rightarrow$ ADP + P

NADPH $\rightarrow$ NADP$^+$ + H$^+$ + 2 electrons

CO_2 $\rightarrow$ $C_6H_{12}O_6$

End products of the dark stage:

The four end products of the dark stage are: glucose, ADP, phosphate and NADP$^+$.

- Glucose may be used to supply energy (in respiration) or it may be converted into starch (for storage), cellulose (for cell walls) or a range of other substances needed by the plant.
- The other three end products (ADP, phosphate and NADP$^+$) are reused in the light phase to form ATP and NADPH, respectively.

Summary of the events in the light and dark stage

Light stage

- Light energy is absorbed.
- Light energy is transferred to electrons.
- The electrons flow along pathways 1 and 2.
- In pathway 1, ATP is formed.
- In pathway 2, water is split and O_2, ATP and NADPH are made.

Dark stage

- Glucose is formed.
- NADPH and ATP are used.

11 Respiration

Learning objectives

In this chapter you will learn about:

1. What is respiration?
2. Energy carriers
3. Aerobic respiration
4. Anaerobic respiration
5. Bioprocessing with immobilised cells

What is respiration?

***Respiration* is the release of energy from food using enzymes.**

The process of respiration is also called cell, internal or tissue respiration. Respiration normally involves the breakdown of glucose. The energy that is released is trapped in the bond between the last two phosphates in ATP. This energy can be used by the cell for different reactions when ATP is later broken down.

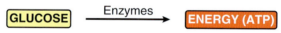

Summary of respiration

Energy carriers

ADP and ATP are dealt with in Chapter 10.

NAD and NADH

NAD^+ is a low-energy molecule involved in respiration. It can combine with two high-energy electrons and a single proton (also called a hydrogen ion or H^+) to form NADH. This reaction can be shown as:

$$NAD^+ + 2e^- + H^+ \rightarrow NADH$$

When NADH breaks down it releases two high-energy electrons and a hydrogen ion (also called a proton).

$$NADH \rightarrow NAD^+ + 2e^- + H^+$$

Aerobic respiration

Aerobic respiration **is the controlled release of energy from food using oxygen.**

The balanced equation for aerobic respiration is:

$$C_6H_{12}O_6 + 6O_2 \xrightarrow{\text{Enzymes}} 6CO_2 + 6H_2O + \text{energy}$$

Aerobic respiration:

- Uses oxygen
- Is an efficient method of releasing energy from food
- Involves a complete breakdown of glucose
- Has two stages (stage 1 and stage 2).

Stage 1

- Takes place in the cytosol of the cell (this is the liquid in the cell that surrounds the cell organelles)
- Does not use oxygen (it is anaerobic)
- Releases very little energy (only 2 ATP molecules for each glucose molecule broken down)
- Converts glucose into two 3-carbon molecules called pyruvic acid
- Converts 2 ADPs into 2 ATPs
- Converts 2 NAD^+ into 2 NADH
- Is also called glycolysis.

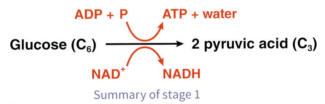

Summary of stage 1

Stage 2

- Takes place in mitochondria
- Requires oxygen (it is aerobic)
- Releases a lot of energy (it produces many ATP molecules)
- Involves both Krebs cycle and the electron transport system
- Krebs cycle makes NADHs and ATP
- The electron transport system converts the energy in NADH to ATPs.

Details of stage 2

Each pyruvic acid (C_3) molecule moves into a mitochondrion, where it loses a carbon dioxide and is converted into acetyl co-enzyme A (which is a two-carbon compound). Acetyl co-enzyme A enters a series of reactions called Krebs cycle.

Krebs cycle

In Krebs cycle acetyl co-enzyme A is broken down to form carbon dioxide and water. Energy-rich electrons are released. These electrons are picked up by NAD$^+$ and used to form NADH. In addition ADP is converted to ATP.

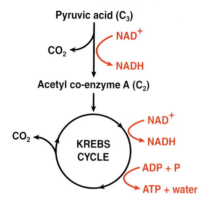

Electron transport system

The NADHs formed in Krebs cycle move to the inner membrane of the mitochondrion where they break down to release the high-energy electrons. These electrons pass along a series of chemicals or electron carriers that form an electron transport system (or chain).

The energy released by the electrons as they pass along the system is used to convert ADPs to ATPs. At the end of the electron transport system the electrons combine with oxygen and hydrogen ions to form water.

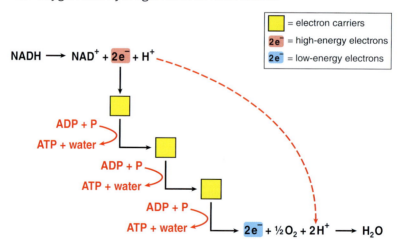

Anaerobic respiration

Anaerobic respiration is the controlled release of energy from food without the use of oxygen. Anaerobic respiration is also called fermentation. There are two main types of anaerobic respiration, each producing different end products.

Lactic acid fermentation

Humans normally carry out aerobic respiration. However, when we are short of oxygen, we carry out lactic acid fermentation. This is shown by the word equation:

Glucose → 2 lactic acid

- The benefit of anaerobic respiration for humans is it supplies a small amount of extra energy.
- The disadvantage is it produces lactic acid, which causes muscles to cramp.

Alcohol fermentation

Yeast and some bacteria carry out alcohol fermentation. This is shown by the word equation:

Glucose → 2 ethanol + 2 carbon dioxide

Both forms of anaerobic respiration may occur in the presence of oxygen, but they do not **use** oxygen.

Anaerobic respiration

- Releases small amounts of energy (in the form of ATP)
- Is an incomplete breakdown of glucose
- Involves only stage 1
- Takes place in the cytosol.

Stages in anaerobic respiration

Anaerobic respiration does not use oxygen. As oxygen is involved in stage 2 this means that anaerobic respiration is a stage 1 process and takes place in the cytosol. Recall that stage 1 (or glycolysis) may be represented as follows.

$$\text{ADP + P} \qquad \text{ATP + water}$$
$$\text{Glucose (C}_6) \longrightarrow \text{2 pyruvic acid (C}_3)$$
$$\text{NAD}^+ \qquad \text{NADH}$$

In anaerobic respiration, pyruvic acid is converted to either lactic acid or ethanol and carbon dioxide. Anaerobic respiration may be summarised as follows.

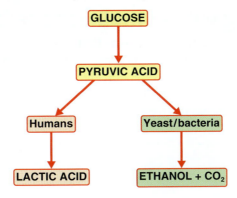

Micro-organisms in industrial fermentations

Fermentation is anaerobic respiration. However, in industry the word 'fermentation' is used to describe the production of useful products by micro-organisms with or without the use of oxygen.

Bioprocessing or *biotechnology* is the production of useful products by living things or their products.

A *bioreactor* is a vessel in which cells or enzymes produce useful products.

Industrial fermentations are carried out in bioreactors. To ensure that the product is properly formed, the following conditions must be applied to a bioreactor.

Conditions needed in bioreactors

- The correct nutrients (e.g. carbohydrates, amino acids, vitamins, minerals, etc.) and micro-organisms must be added.
- A suitable temperature.
- A suitable pH.
- Oxygen may or may not be required.
- A sterile environment must be provided (this means there are no contaminating bacteria or fungi, which grow too fast and produce toxic waste products).
- The mixture is normally stirred or agitated.

Micro-organisms used in bioprocessing:

A wide (and growing) range of micro-organisms is used to produce a huge range of useful chemicals and materials.

- **Historically**, yeast has been used in beer and wine production. Yeast has also been used to supply carbon dioxide to cause the dough to rise in bread-making.
- In the **last century** bacteria and yeasts were first used to manufacture products such as yoghurt, cheese, vinegar, soy sauce and antibiotics.
- In **recent years** bacteria, yeasts and other fungi have been genetically altered (using genetic engineering techniques) to produce a wide range of products such as solvents, amino acids, vitamins, drugs, food additives, enzymes to break down stains, fuel such as biogas and flavourings.

Bioprocessing with immobilised cells

Cells are immobilised in much the same way that enzymes are immobilised (see Chapter 9.) This means that cells such as yeast are mixed with sodium alginate. The yeast/alginate mixture is then left in calcium chloride, which causes the alginate to form beads around the yeast. This immobilises the yeast cells. The pores in the beads are too small for the yeast to pass out but are big enough for any substrate and product to enter or leave.

Use of immobilised cells:

Immobilised cells are widely used to produce many of the modern bioprocessed products listed earlier. In particular, immobilised cells are often used instead of immobilised enzymes (which are more difficult and expensive to prepare).

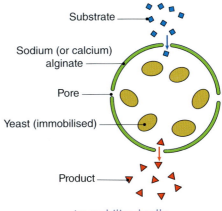

Immobilised cells

Experiment

To prepare and show the production of alcohol by yeast

To prepare alcohol

1   Dissolve some glucose in water.

2   Boil the solution for 5 minutes. *(This removes oxygen from the water to allow anaerobic respiration to occur.)*

3   Allow the boiled glucose solution to cool *(so that the yeast will not be killed)*, and stir in some dried yeast.

4   Cover the solution with oil *(to prevent oxygen from diffusing back into the solution).*

5   Add an air (or fermentation) lock containing water or limewater. *(This allows CO_2 bubbles to pass out but prevents contaminating micro-organisms from entering. Limewater turns milky in the presence of CO_2.)*

6   Place the apparatus in a water bath at 25°C. *(This is an ideal temperature for yeast enzymes.)*

7   Leave for a few days or until there are no more bubbles. *(This means fermentation is completed.)*

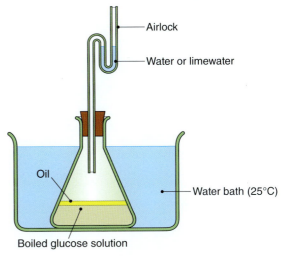

Testing for product

1   Filter the product *(to remove the brown-coloured yeast cells).*

Top Tip!

You need to know how to test the product **either** for ethanol or for alcohol.

2   Test the product for **ethanol** as follows (this is called the iodoform test):
   - Put some of the filtered product into a test tube.
   - Add an equal volume of potassium iodide solution.
   - Add sodium hypochlorite solution. (Note that the solution initially turns a brown-orange colour but then quickly turns clear.)
   - Place the test tube in a hot-water bath.
   - The appearance of pale yellow crystals shows that **ethanol** is present.

3   Test the product for **alcohol** as follows:
   - Put a few drops of orange-coloured acidified potassium (or sodium) dichromate into a test tube.
   - Add some of the filtered product.
   - Place the test tube in a beaker of very hot water.
   - Potassium dichromate turns from orange to green in the presence of alcohol. (This was the old breathalyser test. EU regulations state that dichromate solutions should no longer be used in schools. However, this test is still recognised as a valid answer.)

Diffusion and Osmosis   12

Learning objectives

In this chapter you will learn about:

1   Diffusion
2   Selectively (semi-) permeable membranes
3   Osmosis
4   Osmosis in plant cells
5   Osmosis in animal cells
6   Osmosis and food preservation

Diffusion

Diffusion **is the movement of the molecules of a liquid or a gas from a region of high concentration to a region of low concentration.**

Diffusion is a passive process. This means it does not need an external source of energy.

Examples of diffusion:

1   The molecules in smells such as perfumes or stink bombs spread out by diffusion.

2   If a cell uses oxygen in respiration, it will have a low concentration of oxygen. If the concentration of oxygen outside the cell is higher, oxygen will diffuse into the cell.

3   If a leaf is carrying out photosynthesis, it will be producing oxygen. The concentration of oxygen in the leaf will be high. If the concentration of oxygen in the leaf is higher than the concentration of oxygen in the outside air, oxygen will diffuse out of the leaf.

Selectively (semi-) permeable membranes

- All membranes in biology are similar. This means that the cell membrane is similar to the membranes around a mitochondrion, chloroplast or the nucleus. All these membranes are selectively or semi-permeable. **A selectively permeable membrane allows some molecules to pass through but not others.**
- Water, oxygen and carbon dioxide are molecules that can pass easily across membranes.
- Salts, sugars and proteins are molecules that cannot easily pass across membranes.

Osmosis

Osmosis is the movement of water molecules from a high water concentration to a low water concentration across a semi-permeable membrane.

> **Top Tip!**
>
> **Osmosis** means water moves towards a more concentrated solution.

Comparing diffusion and osmosis:

- Both diffusion and osmosis involve the movement of molecules from high to low concentrations. This means that both processes are passive.
- The difference between them is that osmosis **requires** a semi-permeable membrane while diffusion does not. This means that osmosis is a special case of diffusion.

Experiment

To demonstrate osmosis

1. Soak a length of visking tubing in water. *(Visking tubing is a semi-permeable membrane. Soaking it makes it soft and pliable.)*

2. Tie a knot at one end of the visking tubing.

3. Fill the tubing with a concentrated sucrose, starch or salt solution. *(Each of these molecules is too big to pass through the tubing.)*

4. Tie a knot at the other end of the visking tubing.

5. Dry the tubing and weigh it. Notice how 'full' (or turgid) the tubing feels.

6. Place the tubing in a beaker of distilled water (tap or fresh water can also be used), as shown in the diagram.

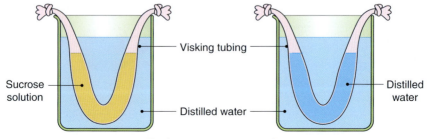

To demonstrate osmosis

7   Repeat steps 1 to 6 but this time fill the visking tubing with distilled water. *(This will act as a control.)*

8   Leave each apparatus for at least 30 minutes.

9   Remove the tubes from the water, dry them and weigh them. Note how 'full' each tube feels.

10   Results:

- The tubing with the concentrated sucrose solution expands and becomes 'fuller' (or more turgid). It also gains in weight. This happens because water moves (due to osmosis) from a high water concentration in the beaker to a low water concentration in the visking tubing.
- The tubing with the distilled water (the control) does not expand, become 'fuller' or gain weight.

Osmosis in plant cells

Plant cells are surrounded by a strong cellulose cell wall. The cell wall is permeable (or fully permeable). This means that both large and small molecules can pass in or out through a cell wall. Plant cells also contain a cell membrane. This is located inside the cell wall. Cell membranes are semi-permeable.

Plant cells with contents that are **more** concentrated than their surroundings

- The cytoplasm of plant cells contains salts, starch, sugars, proteins and other molecules dissolved in water.
- If a plant cell is placed in distilled water, rainwater, fresh water, tap water or a solution that is less concentrated (or more dilute) than its cytoplasm, water will move into the cell due to osmosis. This is the way root cells absorb water from the soil.
- The water will pass into the vacuole (or vacuoles). The cytoplasm and vacuole will swell and the cell membrane will be forced against the cell wall. The cell is now much stronger or firmer due to turgor pressure. The cell is said to be turgid.

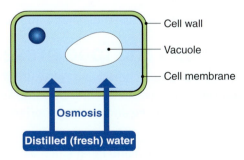

A plant cell in distilled water

- This can be compared to air being forced into a car tyre. The air will inflate the tube against the tyre and make the tyre much stronger.

***Turgor* or *turgor pressure* is the pressure of the vacuole and cytoplasm against the cell wall.**

Plant cells with contents that are **less** concentrated than their surroundings

- If plant cells are placed in very concentrated solutions, water will pass out of the vacuoles and cells due to osmosis.
- The cells lose turgor and become much weaker. The cells are said to be plasmolysed.
- If plant cells lose turgor, the plant will be seen to wilt. This is a temporary process and can be reversed by placing the cells in a less concentrated solution than their cell contents, i.e. water them with tap water.

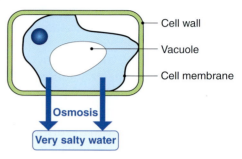

A plant cell in distilled water

Osmosis in animal cells

Animal cells with contents that are **more** concentrated than their surroundings

- If animal cells, such as red blood cells, are placed in very dilute solutions, water will enter the cells due to osmosis.
- The cells will expand and may burst as they do not have a cell wall to restrain them.

Animal cells with contents that are **less** concentrated than their surroundings

- If animal cells are placed in very concentrated solutions, water will pass out of the cells.
- The cells will lose their shape and become shrivelled.

Osmosis and food preservation

Bacteria and fungi both have cell walls. If they are placed in very concentrated solutions, they will lose water by osmosis. This stops enzyme action and prevents them from growing and causing food to decay. There are two main examples of this process.

1   Soaking fish and meat (such as bacon) in very salty solutions preserves them.
2   The high sugar content in jams and marmalade preserves them from fungus decay.

Cell Division

13

Learning objectives

In this chapter you will learn about:

1 Cell continuity

2 Chromosomes

3 Haploid and diploid

4 The cell cycle

5 Mitosis

6 Cancer

7 Meiosis

Cell continuity

Cell continuity is the way in which cells give rise to new cells as a result of cell division.

Chromosomes

- Chromosomes are structures found in the nucleus of the cell. Each chromosome is made of about 60% protein and 40% DNA. The DNA (deoxyribonucleic acid) is wrapped around the protein.

- When cells are not dividing, the chromosomes are elongated into a thread-like material called **chromatin**.

- At cell division the chromatin contracts to form clearly visible rod-shaped structures called chromosomes.

- Genes are located along the length of each chromosome. Each gene is a section of DNA that controls the production of a particular protein.

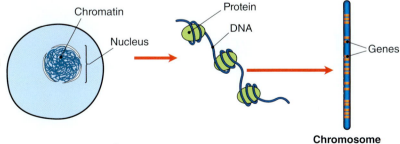

The relationship between chromatin, chromosomes, genes, DNA and protein

- Each species has a particular number of chromosomes in each nucleus. For example, normal human cells have 46 chromosomes.

Haploid and diploid

A *haploid* cell has one of each type of chromosome, i.e. it has a single set of chromosomes.

- The letter 'n' is used to represent haploid.
- The total number of chromosomes in a haploid cell may be given as n = 2. This means the cell has one of each type of chromosome and there are a total of two chromosomes in the cell. In this case the haploid number is 2.
- Human sperm and egg cells are haploid. In each case n = 23 (the haploid number is 23).
- A range of haploid cells is shown in the following diagrams.

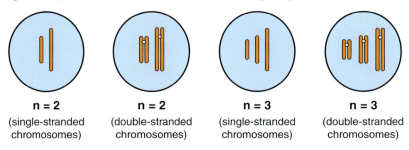

| n = 2 | n = 2 | n = 3 | n = 3 |
| (single-stranded chromosomes) | (double-stranded chromosomes) | (single-stranded chromosomes) | (double-stranded chromosomes) |

Haploid cells

A *diploid* cell has two of each type of chromosome, i.e. it has two sets of chromosomes.

- Diploid is represented as 2n.
- Normal human cells have a diploid number of 46, i.e. 2n = 46.
- A range of diploid cells is shown in the following diagrams.

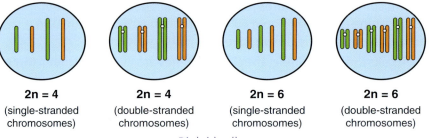

| 2n = 4 | 2n = 4 | 2n = 6 | 2n = 6 |
| (single-stranded chromosomes) | (double-stranded chromosomes) | (single-stranded chromosomes) | (double-stranded chromosomes) |

Diploid cells

The cell cycle

The *cell cycle* describes the events in the life of a cell.

When a cell is first formed, it grows in size. The nucleus then divides (by mitosis or meiosis) followed by cell division to form new cells.

Interphase refers to the time when the cell is not dividing, i.e. most of the time.

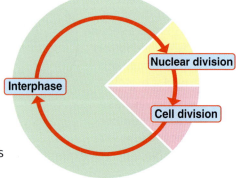

Interphase is a very active phase (even though the cell is not dividing).

- During early interphase new cell organelles are being formed.
- In late interphase each chromosome forms an identical copy of itself, i.e. DNA replication takes place.

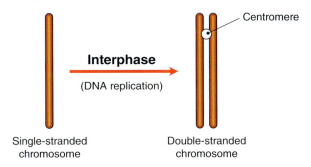

Mitosis

***Mitosis* is a form of nuclear division in which a nucleus forms two nuclei containing identical sets of chromosomes.**

Mitosis can be divided into four phases:

1. Prophase
2. Metaphase
3. Anaphase
4. Telophase

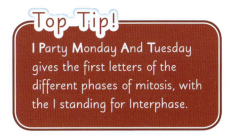

Top Tip!

I Party **M**onday **A**nd **T**uesday gives the first letters of the different phases of mitosis, with the **I** standing for Interphase.

The following diagrams represent mitosis in an animal cell with four chromosomes, i.e. 2n = 4.

Prophase

- In late interphase and early prophase, chromatin starts to contract.
- Chromosomes become visible as double-stranded structures held together by a centromere. The two strands in a chromosome contain identical genes.
- The nuclear membrane breaks down.
- Spindle fibres start to form later in prophase.

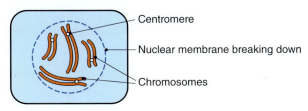

Metaphase

- Chromosomes line up along the equator of the cell.
- Two spindle fibres attach to each centromere.

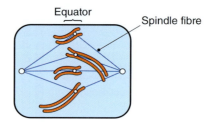

Anaphase

- The spindle fibres contract.
- The centromeres break; each chromosome is pulled apart, with opposite strands pulled to each pole of the cell (the strands are called chromosomes at this stage).
- This means that the four chromosomes pulled to each pole are identical to each other.

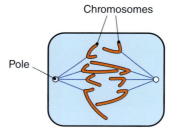

Telophase

- The chromosomes elongate and revert back to chromatin.
- The spindle fibres break down.
- A nuclear membrane forms around each group of four chromosomes.
- The cell divides to form two daughter cells when a groove called the **cleavage furrow** forms in the region where the chromosomes had lined up. The furrow deepens until two cells have formed.
- The two cells formed each have four chromosomes and each cell has identical genes.

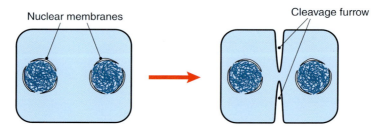

Mitosis in plant cells

The account given so far refers to an animal cell. The events are similar for a plant cell with the following differences.

- A cell wall is present around each plant cell.
- At cell division there is no cleavage furrow. Instead many small membrane-enclosed vesicles collect at the equator of the cell. These vesicles contain cellulose and all the other materials needed to form new cell membranes and walls. The vesicles join to form a **cell plate**. New cell walls form on either side of the cell plate.

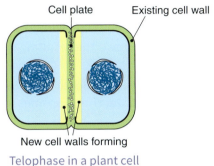

Telophase in a plant cell

Functions of mitosis

1   In single-celled organisms (such as bacteria and amoeba) mitosis increases the number of organisms. In these cases mitosis is a method of **multiplication** or **reproduction**. This form of reproduction is asexual and the cells formed have identical genes.

2   In multi-celled organisms mitosis increases the number of cells. This makes it the basis for growth and repair in multicellular organisms.

Cancer

Cancer is a group of disorders in which certain cells lose their ability to control their rate of mitosis and the number of times mitosis takes place.

There are many different types of cancer but in each case there is an uncontrolled production of abnormal body cells. The uncontrolled growth of cells forms a malignant tumour. These tumours are serious because they:

- Continue to grow out of control
- May invade and damage other cells
- May move and grow in other parts of the body.

Causes of cancer

- Cancer is caused when normal genes are altered or mutated to form cancer-causing genes called oncogenes.

- These alterations (or mutations) are triggered by cancer-causing agents called **carcinogens**. Common carcinogens include:
  - Chemicals, such as cigarette smoke and asbestos fibres
  - Radiation, such as ultraviolet and X-rays
  - Some viruses.

Meiosis

***Meiosis* is a form of nuclear division in which the daughter nuclei contain half the number of chromosomes of the parent nucleus.**

- Meiosis halves the number of chromosomes in the nucleus. This means that haploid cells will form if a diploid cell divides by meiosis.
- If a human cell divides by meiosis the resulting cells will be haploid and contain 23 chromosomes, i.e. n = 23.
- In addition meiosis produces chromosomes with different combinations of genes compared to the parental chromosomes. In this way meiosis produces genetic variation.

Functions of meiosis

1   Meiosis allows the chromosome number to be maintained when two cells (called gametes or sex cells) combine (fertilise) in sexual reproduction.

For example, in humans:

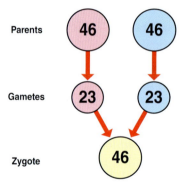

2   Meiosis allows genes to be re-arranged, which gives rise to new variations in organisms produced by sexual reproduction.

Differences between mitosis and meiosis

Mitosis	Meiosis
Maintains the chromosome number	Halves the chromosome number
Produces cells with identical genes	Produces cells with different combinations of genes

Genetics

14

Learning objectives

In this chapter you will learn about:

1 What is a species?
2 Heredity and genes
3 How sex is determined
4 Mendel's laws
5 Linkage
6 Sex linkage
7 Non-nuclear inheritance

What is a species?

A *species* is a group of organisms capable of naturally interbreeding with each other to produce fertile offspring.

The most basic unit of classification is a species. All humans form a single species. Dogs and cats are different species, as are oak and ash trees.

Variation within a species

***Variation* means there are differences between members of the same species.**

The members of a species have many features in common. However, there are also many differences or variations within a species. Variations in a species may be acquired or inherited.

Acquired variations

***Acquired variations* are learned during life.**

Acquired variations are developed during life but are not passed from one generation to the next. Examples: speaking a language, driving a car, walking, speaking and texting.

Inherited variations

***Inherited variations* are controlled by genes and passed on from generation to generation.**

Examples: producing hair, nails, two arms, one liver and forming enzymes and hormones.

Heredity and genes

- *Heredity* **is the passing on of features from parents to offspring by means of genes.** Heredity is also called genetic inheritance.

- **A** *gene* **is a section of DNA that carries the code for the production of a particular protein.**

- *Gene expression* **is the way in which the genetic code contained in a gene is converted into a protein.** It refers to the way in which genes work.

- **A** *gamete* **is a haploid cell capable of fertilisation.** Normal body cells (called somatic cells) are diploid. Gametes or sex cells are formed by meiosis, which converts diploid cells into haploid cells.

- *Fertilisation* **is the union of gametes to form a diploid zygote.**

Genetic crosses

- *Alleles* **are different forms of the same gene.**

  For example, rabbits may have long ears (L) or short ears (l), i.e. the gene for ears has two alleles (or versions): L and l.

- *Dominant* **describes an allele that prevents a recessive allele from working.** *Recessive* **describes an allele that is prevented from working by a dominant allele.**

  A rabbit with the alleles Ll has long ears because the recessive allele for short ears (l) is prevented from working by the dominant allele for long ears (L).

- *Genotype* **means the genetic make-up of an organism.** The possible genotypes for ear length in rabbits are LL, Ll and ll.

- *Phenotype* **means the physical make-up of an organism.** The phenotypes of the rabbits are either long ears or short ears.

  The phenotype is formed by the interaction of the genotype with the environment, i.e. phenotype = genotype + environment.

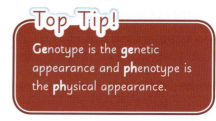

Top Tip!

Genotype is the **ge**netic appearance and **ph**enotype is the **ph**ysical appearance.

- *Homozygous* **means that both the alleles are the same.**

  The genotypes LL and ll are both homozygous.

- *Heterozygous* **means that the alleles are different.**

  The genotype Ll is heterozygous.

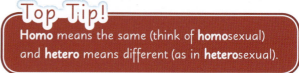

Top Tip!

Homo means the same (think of **homo**sexual) and **hetero** means different (as in **hetero**sexual).

Question 1

In rabbits, long ears (L) are dominant over short ears (l). Show the genotypes and phenotypes for the offspring of a cross between two rabbits whose genotypes are LL and ll.

Answer 1

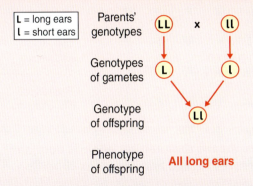

L = long ears	
l = short ears	

Parents' genotypes

Genotypes of gametes

Genotype of offspring

Phenotype of offspring — **All long ears**

Question 2

Freckles (F) are dominant over no freckles (f). Use a Punnett square to show the possible genotypes and phenotypes of the progeny of a cross between two parents who are heterozygous for this trait.

Answer 2

A Punnett square is a grid used to show the genotypes of the gametes and offspring in a genetic cross. Progeny is another word for offspring.

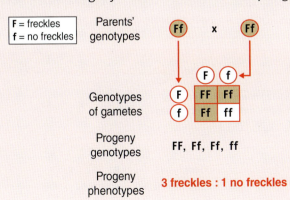

F = freckles	
f = no freckles	

Parents' genotypes

Genotypes of gametes

Progeny genotypes — **FF, Ff, Ff, ff**

Progeny phenotypes — **3 freckles : 1 no freckles**

Question 3

In a species of plant, round seed (R) is dominant over wrinkled seed (r). What is the percentage chance of a homozygous dominant plant and a heterozygous plant producing a round-seeded plant in the F$_1$ generation?

Answer 3

The F$_1$ generation is the first filial generation. This means the first generation of offspring produced by the parents.

As seen in the cross, there is a 100% chance of a round-seeded plant being produced.

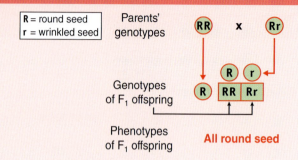

R = round seed
r = wrinkled seed

Parents' genotypes

Genotypes of F$_1$ offspring

Phenotypes of F$_1$ offspring

All round seed

Incomplete dominance **means that neither allele is dominant or recessive. Both alleles work (are expressed) in the heterozygous condition.**

Snapdragon flowers are an example of incomplete dominance.

In snapdragons:

RR = red petals

Rr = pink petals (not red petals)

rr = white petals

Question 4

In snapdragons, flower colour is controlled by the alleles R and r. The intermediate condition (Rr) gives pink flowers. Using a Punnett square, show the genotypes and phenotypes of a cross between two pink-flowered snapdragons.

Answer 4

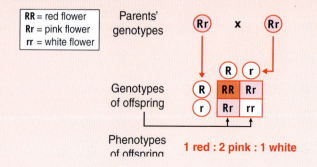

RR = red flower
Rr = pink flower
rr = white flower

Parents' genotypes

Genotypes of offspring

Phenotypes of offspring

1 red : 2 pink : 1 white

Question 5

In humans, normal skin pigment (N) is dominant over albinism (n). Show the genotypes and phenotypes of the F_2 generation for a cross between two homozygous parents, one with normal skin pigment and the other with albinism.

Top Tip!

To get to the F_2 generation you must cross (or self) two F_1 progeny. This means you cross an F_1 genotype with another F_1 genotype.

Answer 5

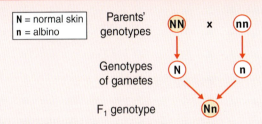

N = normal skin
n = albino

Parents' genotypes: NN × nn

Genotypes of gametes: N   n

F_1 genotype: Nn

We now cross an F_1 with an F_1 to get to the F_2 generation.

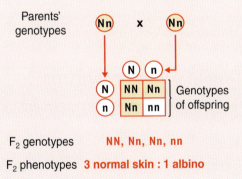

Parents' genotypes: Nn × Nn

	N	n
N	NN	Nn
n	Nn	nn

Genotypes of offspring

F_2 genotypes   NN, Nn, Nn, nn

F_2 phenotypes **3 normal skin : 1 albino**

How sex is determined

Normal body (somatic) cells in humans contain 46 chromosomes.

Forty-four of these chromosomes have genes that do not control sexuality.

The two remaining chromosomes are called sex chromosomes. These chromosomes (called the X and Y chromosome) control sexuality.

- Male body cells are XY.
- Female body cells are XX.

This arrangement has two consequences:

- It is the father who determines the sex of a child.
- The ratio of male to female births is 1:1.

With the help of diagrams show why in humans it is the father who determines the sex of a child.

Answer 6

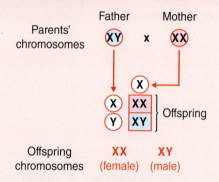

In the previous cross the mother always gives an X chromosome to her offspring. The sex of the offspring depends on the type of sperm that fertilises the egg.

- A sperm with an X chromosome produces a female child.
- A sperm with a Y chromosome produces a male child.

Sex determination in other organisms

Birds, moths and butterflies have the reverse arrangement for sexuality. In these organisms:

- Male body cells are XX.
- Female body cells are XY.

In these organisms it is the **female** who determines the sex of the offspring.

Mendel's laws

Gregor Mendel is known as the father of genetics. He was an Augustinian monk who carried out numerous crosses in the mid-1800s. He worked mainly on garden pea plants. His work led to two laws.

***Mendel's first law** (the law of segregation) states that:*

- **Inherited characteristics are controlled by pairs of factors**
- **These factors segregate at gamete formation so that only one factor is carried in each gamete.**

What Mendel called factors are now called alleles. Mendel predicted that alleles occurred in pairs (i.e. cells were diploid) and some process (now known to be meiosis) resulted in the number of alleles being halved.

Example of Mendel's law of segregation

- Freckles are controlled by two alleles F and f. At meiosis these alleles separate and only one allele is carried in each gamete:

Parent cell

Gametes

- In terms of chromosomes Mendel's law of segregation also applies.

Alleles are located on chromosomes. If there are two alleles there must be two chromosomes. Meiosis ensures that only one chromosome (containing a single allele) is carried in each gamete, as shown below.

Chromosomes in parent cell

Chromosomes in gametes

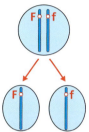

Mendel's second law (the law of independent assortment) states that:

- **At gamete formation either member of a pair of factors is equally likely to recombine with either of another pair of factors.**

The word 'alleles' can be substituted for the word 'factors' in this definition.

Example of Mendel's law of independent assortment

- If a cell has the genotype PpTt, each of the following gamete types is equally likely to be formed: PT, Pt, pT, pt.

Parent cell

- This law can be shown in terms of chromosome diagrams as shown:

Gametes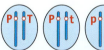

Point to note

Monohybrid and dihybrid crosses

A **monohybrid** cross involves only one trait.

For example a cross that involves petal colour or the presence or absence of freckles. All the crosses in this chapter so far have been monohybrid crosses.

Dihybrid crosses involve two traits.

(Question 7 (overleaf) is a dihybrid cross as it involves coat colour **and** length of whiskers.)

Question 7

In mice, brown coat (B) is dominant over white coat (b). In addition, long whiskers (L) are dominant over short whiskers (l).

Show the genotypes and phenotypes of the F_1 progeny for a cross between a brown-coated, long-whiskered mouse (heterozygous for both traits) and a white-coated, short-whiskered mouse.

Answer 7

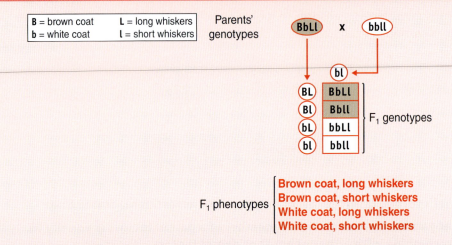

	B = brown coat	L = long whiskers
	b = white coat	l = short whiskers

Parents' genotypes: BbLl x bbll

F_1 genotypes:

	bl
BL	BbLl
Bl	Bbll
bL	bbLl
bl	bbll

F_1 phenotypes:
Brown coat, long whiskers
Brown coat, short whiskers
White coat, long whiskers
White coat, short whiskers

Question 8

In pea plants, purple flowers are dominant over white flowers. In addition, round pods are dominant over constricted pods. Show the results of the F_2 generation of a cross involving a plant with purple flowers and round pods (homozygous for both traits) and a plant with white flowers and constricted pods.

Answer 8

When letters are not given, it is normal to use the first letter of the dominant trait, e.g. P and R.

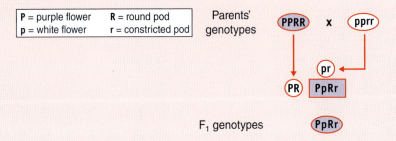

	P = purple flower	R = round pod
	p = white flower	r = constricted pod

Parents' genotypes: PPRR x pprr

	pr
PR	PpRr

F_1 genotypes: PpRr

To get to the F_2 you cross two F_1 genotypes, i.e. PpRr x PpRr

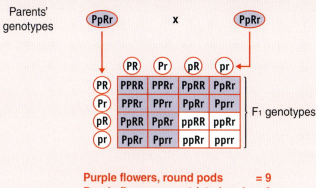

Parents' genotypes

PpRr   x   PpRr

	PR	Pr	pR	pr
PR	PPRR	PPRr	PpRR	PpRr
Pr	PPRr	PPrr	PpRr	Pprr
pR	PpRR	PpRr	ppRR	ppRr
pr	PpRr	Pprr	ppRr	pprr

F_1 genotypes

F_1 phenotypes

Purple flowers, round pods	= 9
Purple flowers, constricted pods	= 3
White flowers, round pods	= 3
White flowers, constricted pods	= 1

Linkage

***Linkage* means that genes are located on the same chromosome.** Linked genes are passed on together to the next generation.

The *locus* is the position of a gene on a chromosome (plural = loci). The locus is usually shown on a chromosome diagram as shown.

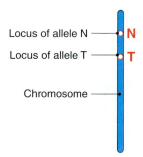

Examples of linked genes

Example 1

In the diagram shown on the right:

- There are two chromosomes
- There are two sets of linked alleles, i.e. A and B along with a and b
- The genotype is AaBb.

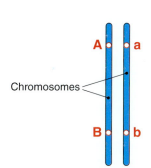

Example 2

In the example on the right:

- There are four chromosomes
- The alleles S and T along with s and t are linked
- Neither of the P alleles is linked to anything
- The genotype is SsTtPP.

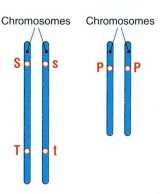

Question 9

A cell has the genotype KkLl and the dominant alleles are linked. Draw a simple chromosome diagram to show this cell. Draw diagrams to show the genotypes of the gametes produced by this cell.

Answer 9

The cell shown above has the genotype KkLl and the genes **are linked**. The cell produces only two types of gametes (i.e. KL and kl, as shown).

Cell =

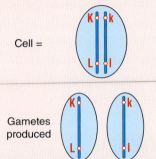

If a cell has the same genotype (KkLl) but the genes are **not linked** then, according to Mendel's second law, there are four types of gametes produced (i.e. KL, Kl, kL, kl). This means that **linkage contradicts Mendel's second law**. An example of this is shown in question 10.

Gametes produced

Question 10

Show the results of the following cross: AaBb x aabb

(a) If the genes are not linked

(b) If the genes are linked.

Answer 10

(a)

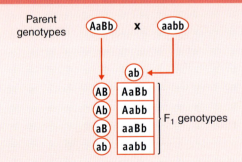

Parent genotypes

	ab
AB	AaBb
Ab	Aabb
aB	aaBb
ab	aabb

F$_1$ genotypes

The four genotypes shown in the Punnett square will occur with equal frequency, i.e. the ratio will be 1:1:1:1.

(b)

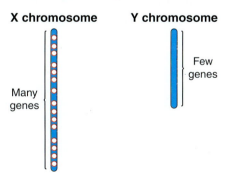

Parent genotypes

F₁ genotypes

In this case only **two** types of gamete are formed from the heterozygous parent cell (in contradiction of Mendel's second law). As a result only two types of offspring phenotypes are produced.

Sex linkage

Sex linked means that traits are controlled by genes located on the sex (or X) chromosome.

Examples of sex-linked traits in humans are red–green colour blindness and haemophilia (the inability to form blood clots).

In humans the sex chromosomes are the X and Y chromosomes. The X chromosome is a normal chromosome and contains many genes. The Y chromosome is a very short chromosome and contains very few genes.

X chromosome   Y chromosome

Many genes

Few genes

Any gene located on a sex chromosome is almost certain to be to be on the X chromosome (as there are so few genes on the Y chromosome). This means that sex-linked (also called X-linked) traits are most likely to be seen in males. This is explained in question 11 (overleaf).

Explain by means of diagrams why red–green colour blindness is more likely to affect males.

Possible female genotypes:

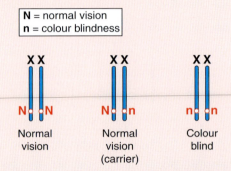

A female must have **two** recessive alleles to be colour blind. Since recessive alleles are rare it is very unlikely that a female would have two of them.

Possible male genotypes:

A male only needs **one** allele for any sex-linked trait. This means it is more likely that a male will suffer from sex-linked traits (such as colour blindness).

Question 12

In the fruit fly, eye colour is a sex-linked trait. Red eye (R) is dominant over white eye (r). Show the results of a cross between two red-eyed flies, with the female parent being heterozygous for the trait.

Answer 12

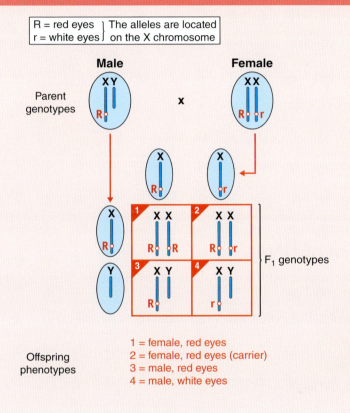

R = red eyes	The alleles are located
r = white eyes	on the X chromosome

Parent genotypes

Offspring phenotypes

1 = female, red eyes
2 = female, red eyes (carrier)
3 = male, red eyes
4 = male, white eyes

Non-nuclear inheritance

- The vast majority of genes are located on chromosomes in the nucleus.
- However, a small number of genes are also found on DNA located in mitochondria and chloroplasts. These genes are not inherited in the nucleus.
- A sperm cell does not pass any mitochondria to the zygote. However, the mitochondria in the egg are passed on to the zygote. This means we inherit our mitochondria from our mothers. Any genes on the mitochondrial DNA are passed on only from the mother.

15 DNA and RNA

Learning objectives

In this chapter you will learn about:

1 Structure of DNA

2 DNA replication

3 The genetic code

4 DNA profiles

5 Genetic screening

6 RNA

7 Protein synthesis

Structure of DNA

DNA (deoxyribonucleic acid) is a very long coiled molecule. There are about 3 m of DNA in every human cell.

The structure of DNA can be considered under three headings:

1 Nucleotides

2 Base pairs

3 The double helix.

Nucleotides

A *nucleotide* consists of a phosphate group, a sugar and a nitrogen-containing base. The sugar used in DNA is called deoxyribose.

There are four different bases:

Adenine (A), thymine (T), guanine (G) and cytosine (C).

- Adenine and guanine are called purines.
- Thymine and cytosine are called pyrimidines.

Top Tip!

The rules about purines and pyrimidines can be recalled using the following phrases:

The **A**ttorney **G**eneral is **p**ure.

The bases with 'y' are **py**rimidines.

There are four DNA nucleotides:

P—D—A   **P—D—G**   **P—D—C**   **P—D—T**

(P = phosphate, D = deoxyribose)

DNA nucleotides

Base (or nucleotide) pairs

Adenine and thymine both form **two** weak hydrogen bonds. This allows them to join together. They are said to form a complementary base pair. In the same way guanine and cytosine form **three** hydrogen bonds and are another complementary base pair.

DNA is made of a sequence of base pairs linked by hydrogen bonds. Note that in each base pair there is a purine–pyrimidine link. The complementary strands have phosphates on the outside; the deoxyribose sugars are next, with the bases on the inside.

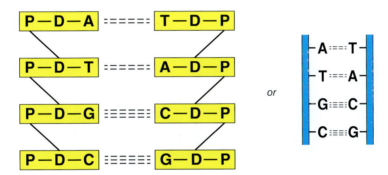

or

At this level of structure DNA resembles a ladder, as shown in the diagram.

The double helix

In 1953 James Watson and Francis Crick proposed that DNA was in fact a double helix.

This means that the double-stranded DNA molecule is wound into a double spiral, as shown in the diagram.

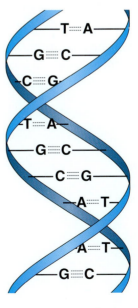

The structure of DNA

To isolate DNA from a plant tissue

1 Mix some salt and washing-up liquid in water. *(The washing-up liquid will break down the membranes while the salt will cause DNA to clump.)*

2 Chop an onion or kiwi fruit into small pieces and add the pieces to the salt/detergent solution. *(The onion or kiwi will provide a source of DNA.)*

3 Leave the onion/salt/detergent mixture in a water bath at 60°C for 15 minutes. *(This temperature will inactivate enzymes that damage DNA.)*

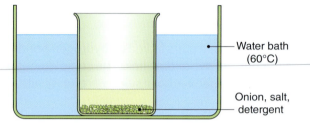

Water bath (60°C)

Onion, salt, detergent

4 Remove the mixture from the hot water and place it in an ice-cold water bath. *(This will prevent the breakdown of DNA.)*

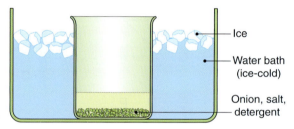

Ice

Water bath (ice-cold)

Onion, salt, detergent

5 Blend the mixture for 4 seconds in a food blender. *(This breaks down the cell walls but the short duration does not harm DNA.)*

6 Filter the mixture through coffee filter paper. *(This allows DNA and proteins but not cell parts to pass through; the pores in normal filter paper are too small to allow this to happen fast enough.)*

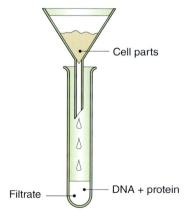

Cell parts

Filtrate

DNA + protein

7   Place some of the filtrate in a test tube and add a few drops of protease enzyme. *(The protease will break down the proteins around the DNA.)*

8   Pour some ice-cold (from the freezer) ethanol down the side of the test tube so that it forms a layer on top of the filtrate. *(DNA rises from the filtrate. DNA is insoluble in ice-cold ethanol and remains at the ethanol–filtrate boundary.)*

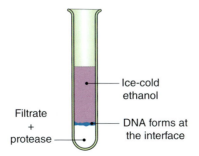

Ice-cold
ethanol

Filtrate
+
protease

DNA forms at
the interface

9   Gently twist a small wire loop or glass rod at the boundary between the ethanol and the filtrate. *(DNA is seen as a clear mesh of white 'mucus' wrapped around the wire or loop.)*

DNA replication

DNA replication takes place in the nucleus of the cell during interphase. It results in a single-stranded chromosome forming two **identical** strands that are held together at the centromere.

The sequence of bases on one strand of a double helix determines the sequence of bases on the complementary strand. For example, if one side of DNA has the base sequence AGGCCTTA, then the other side must be TCCGGAAT.

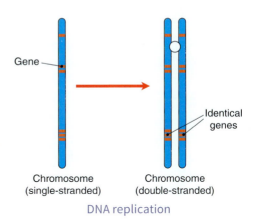

Gene

Identical
genes

Chromosome
(single-stranded)

Chromosome
(double-stranded)

DNA replication

DNA replication occurs as follows:

1   The double helix unwinds.

2   Enzymes break the hydrogen bonds.

3   The complementary strands move apart.

4   DNA nucleotides move from the cytoplasm into the nucleus and attach to their complementary bases on the exposed strands.

5   The new strands contain exactly the same sequence of bases. Each new stretch of DNA re-forms into a double helix.

6 This process is shown in the following diagram for a very short section of DNA.

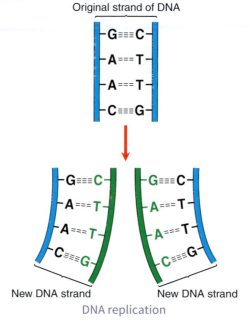

Original strand of DNA

New DNA strand   New DNA strand

DNA replication

Significance of DNA replication

DNA is able to produce **exact copies** of itself. This allows exactly the same DNA to be passed to each daughter cell during mitosis.

The genetic code

Genes are composed of long sequences of DNA bases. Genes cause a sequence of amino acids to be assembled to form a protein. To allow the correct amino acids to be assembled DNA carries a genetic code.

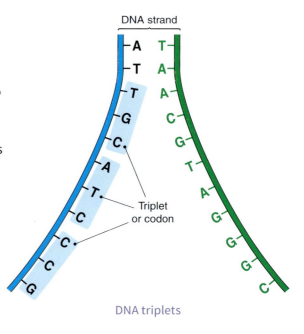

DNA strand

Triplet or codon

DNA triplets

The DNA (or genetic) code operates as a sequence of three DNA bases called a triplet or codon. It takes many triplets to form a gene.

A *triplet* **is a sequence of three bases in a row.**

A *codon* **is a triplet that acts as a code for an amino acid.**

The diagram represents a tiny section of a gene.

Coding and non-coding DNA

- Only about 3% of DNA acts to form proteins.
- About 97% of the DNA in a human nucleus does not cause the production of proteins. While this non-coding (or so-called 'junk') DNA does not code for a protein it is now thought that it acts as a control to switch genes on and off.
- Some of the non-coding DNA is located **between** genes, with a large amount at the centromeres and at the ends of the chromosome. Much of it, however, is found **within** genes.

DNA profiles

A *DNA profile* is a unique pattern of DNA from one person that is compared with the DNA profile of another person. DNA profiling is also called genetic or DNA fingerprinting.

Preparing DNA profiles

1 Release DNA from cells

DNA is released from cells in the same way as in the experiment to isolate DNA from plant tissue. The cells may be obtained from a saliva sample, the root of a hair, or a sample of semen.

2 Cut the DNA into fragments

The DNA is cut into pieces using special enzymes (called restriction enzymes). These enzymes cut DNA when they encounter specific base sequences.

This is similar to cutting a section of text wherever a given word or sequence of words is found. The DNA sections obtained in this way will vary in length from very small sequences of bases to very long sequences.

3 Separate the fragments

The DNA fragments are separated according to their length. This involves placing the fragments in a gel and passing an electric current through the gel.

Small fragments move faster through the gel than large ones. A photograph of the final results is obtained.

Each DNA profile looks like a bar code. The profile (or 'bar code') is different for each person. The likelihood of two people having the same DNA profile or fingerprint is very low (unless they are identical twins).

A typical DNA profile is shown in the diagram.

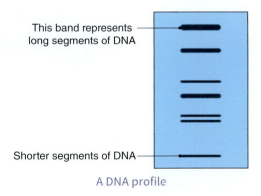

This band represents long segments of DNA

Shorter segments of DNA

A DNA profile

Uses of DNA profiles

Crime

DNA profiles may be used to link somebody to a crime or to the scene of a crime. If some biological tissue (such as saliva on a cigarette butt, a semen stain, or a hair) is found at the crime scene, its DNA profile is compared with one taken from a suspect. If the patterns match, the suspect is associated with the crime scene.

See, for example, the four DNA profiles below: the first is from the crime scene while the others are from suspects.

There is a match between number 1 and number 4.

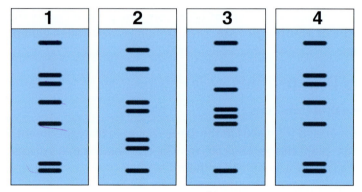

Four DNA profiles

Medical

DNA profiles may be used to establish if a man is the father of a child (i.e. to establish paternity). Paternity cases are important in immigration, inheritance and rape cases. DNA profiles obtained from the mother, child and the man are compared.

If all of the child's bands match either one of the mother's or one of the man's bands, then the man is the father of the child, as shown below.

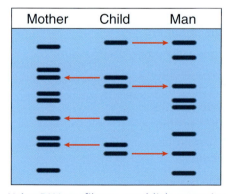

Using DNA profiles to establish paternity

If some of the child's bands match the mother's but the others do not match the man's, then he is not the father of the child, as shown below.

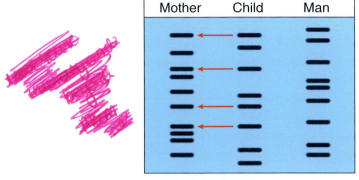

Using DNA profiles to disprove paternity

Genetic screening

Genetic screening means testing a person's DNA for the presence of abnormal or altered DNA.

This process uses some of the techniques associated with DNA profiling.

The presence of abnormal or altered DNA is an indication that a particular gene is mutated.

Mutated genes are the cause of many genetic disorders such as:

- Cystic fibrosis (where fluid cannot be removed from the lungs)
- Haemochromatosis (where there is too much iron in the body)
- Albinism (the inability to form the pigment melanin)

The value of genetic screening

If a couple know that one or both of them have a particular mutation, they can be advised as to the probability that they will have a child affected by the disorder. They can then decide whether or not to have children.

If a child is born with a disorder, it is often helpful to be aware of this possibility in advance so that treatment can begin immediately.

Ethical problems

Genetic screening may cause problems, such as those listed below.

- If an embryo is tested and shown to have a disorder, it may encourage the couple to consider abortion.
- Should a person be told they have a disorder that will develop later in life and lead to death?
- Should insurance companies or potential employers be informed of genetic screening results?

RNA

RNA (ribonucleic acid) differs from DNA, as shown in the following table.

	DNA	RNA
Bases	A, T, G, C (has thymine)	A, U, G, C (has uracil)
Sugar	Deoxyribose	Ribose
Shape	Double helix	Single-stranded
Location	Mainly found in the nucleus	Found in the nucleus and cytosol
Number of types	Only one type	Three types: mRNA, tRNA, rRNA

RNA bases are complementary to DNA bases. For example, if DNA has the base sequence TAGGC, the RNA complementary sequence will be AUCCG.

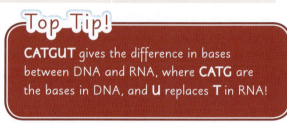

Top Tip!

CATGUT gives the difference in bases between DNA and RNA, where **CATG** are the bases in DNA, and **U** replaces **T** in RNA!

Protein synthesis

Genes control cells by producing enzymes. Enzymes are proteins. To make the correct proteins it is important that amino acids are assembled in the correct order in ribosomes. Genes work (are expressed) by forming the correct proteins.

Protein synthesis involves the genetic code in DNA being transcribed to mRNA and this code being translated into the correct sequence of amino acids. Transcription takes place in the nucleus and translation takes place in the ribosomes.

Transcription **is converting the code on DNA to a code on mRNA.**
Translation **is converting the code from RNA to form protein.**

DNA $\xrightarrow{\text{Transcription}}$ RNA $\xrightarrow{\text{Translation}}$ Protein

The main steps in protein synthesis are as follows:

1. The double helix unwinds at the site of the gene that is to form a protein.

2. The sequence of bases on the DNA (gene) is used to form a complementary strand of messenger RNA (mRNA). This process is called transcription.

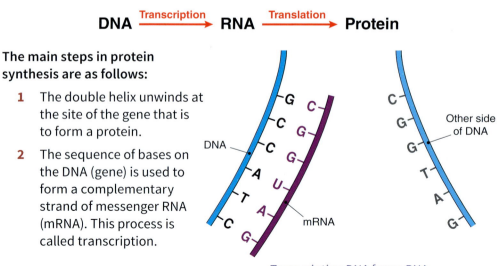

Transcription DNA forms RNA

3   The mRNA strand moves out of the nucleus into the cytoplasm.

4   Ribosomes are made mainly of ribosomal RNA (rRNA).

5   The mRNA strand moves into a ribosome.

6   There are a large number of transfer RNA (tRNA) molecules in the cytoplasm. Each tRNA carries a specific amino acid.

7   Triplets or codons on the mRNA strand attract complementary triplets (called anti-codons) on tRNA molecules.

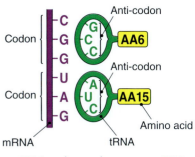

mRNA and complementary tRNA

8   The amino acids are detached from their tRNA molecules and bonded together in the ribosome to form the new protein.

9   The protein then folds into the correct 3D shape to allow it to function properly.

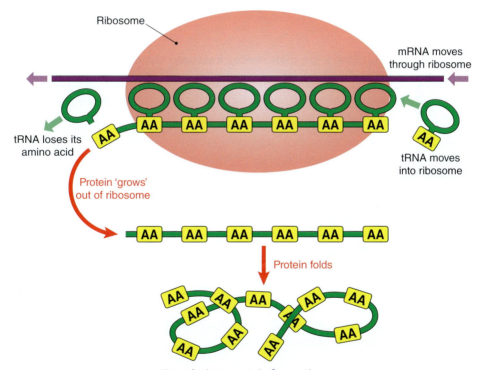

Translation: protein formation

Types of codon

A gene has one start codon, many codons that code for amino acids and one stop codon.

- **Start codon** – This indicates the beginning of the gene.
- **Amino acid codons** – These cause many amino acids to line up in the ribosome to form a protein.
- **Stop codon** – This indicates the end of the gene.

16 Evolution

Learning objectives

In this chapter you will learn about:

1. Variation
2. Evolution
3. Theory of evolution by natural selection
4. Evidence for evolution

Variation

Variation means that there are differences between the members of a species.

Only **inherited (genetic) variations** are considered here. **Acquired variations** are not passed on to the next generation. Genetic variation is caused by sexual reproduction and by mutations.

Mutations

A mutation is a change in the amount or structure of DNA.

Mutations happen naturally when DNA fails to replicate properly. The rate of mutation is normally very low. In addition, DNA has enzymes that repair the vast majority of mutated genes. Mutations occur at random locations on the chromosome.

The change in DNA usually means that a protein cannot be made. This may be a serious problem if the protein is important for the cell. Mutations in somatic (non-reproductive) cells may sometimes be serious (e.g. when they cause cancer). However, mutations in gametes are often very serious (because the mutation may be passed on to all the cells of the offspring).

Causes of mutations

Mutagens are agents that increase the natural rate of mutations.

Mutagens that cause cancer are called carcinogens. Mutagens include:

- Radiation such as X-rays and ultraviolet radiation
- Chemicals such as cigarette smoke, caffeine and formaldehyde.

Types of mutation

- **Gene mutations** affect only small sections of DNA (i.e. only one or a few genes). These mutations cannot be seen (but their effects can be seen). Examples of gene mutations are:
    - Albinism (the inability to produce melanin)
    - Cystic fibrosis (the inability to clear mucus from the lungs and other organs)
    - Sickle-cell anaemia (the inability to form correct haemoglobin).
- **Chromosome mutations** affect large sections of a chromosome or can involve entire chromosomes and sets of chromosomes. An example of a chromosome mutation is:
    - Down syndrome (where a person has 47 chromosomes (instead of 46). This results from a gamete (usually the egg) containing 24 chromosomes combining with a normal gamete with 23 chromosomes.

Evolution

Evolution **is the way in which living things change genetically to produce new species over long periods of time.**

The most commonly accepted theory of evolution was proposed by **Charles Darwin** in 1858. Darwin got many of his ideas when he worked as a scientific officer on board the HMS *Beagle*. This ship sailed around the Galapagos Islands in the 1830s.

Another scientist, **Alfred Russel Wallace**, had come up with the same ideas around the same time. It was Wallace who encouraged Darwin to publish their joint theory.

Theory of evolution by natural selection

Observations	Conclusions
Organisms produce **large numbers of offspring.** For example, trees produce many seeds and rabbits produce large families.	There is a **struggle for existence.** This is now called competition. Animals compete for space, food, water and partners. Plants compete for light, space, water and minerals.
The environment can **support only a limited number of organisms.** For example, there is enough space, food or water to support only a limited number of organisms.	

There are **genetic variations** among the members of a population. These variations arise from sexual reproduction and mutations.	Those organisms that are best suited (adapted) to their environment live on. Provided they reproduce they will pass their genes on to the following generation.
	Those that are not so well adapted die out (which means their genes are not passed on to the next generation). This process is called **natural selection** (or 'survival of the fittest').
	Organisms accumulate many small changes over long periods of time. Some of the organisms move to new locations. Eventually, new species form (i.e. organisms are now so different that they cannot interbreed with the original species). This is called **speciation**.

Evidence for evolution

The main sources of evidence for evolution are fossil studies, comparative adaptations or anatomy, the study of embryos, and genetic evidence.

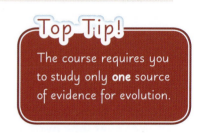

Top Tip!

The course requires you to study only **one** source of evidence for evolution.

The fossil evidence

A fossil is something (or evidence of something) that lived a long time ago.

Examples of fossils include entire organisms preserved in ice, bogs and amber (which is solid resin from trees). Fossils also include bones, teeth, seeds, footprints, stone forests, pollen grains, leaf prints and even solidified faeces.

Fossils support the theory of evolution in the following ways:

- They can be dated, which allows changes to be related to time.
- Some species found as fossils are no longer found alive. Species such as dinosaurs and the giant Irish elk have become extinct.
- Some modern species have no fossil remains. For example, there are no modern human remains found from millions of years ago. This indicates that we have only recently evolved.
- Modern organisms are more complex than their fossil predecessors.
- Changes in the fossil record may be related to environmental changes.

Horse height as an example of fossil evidence

Fossil records of the horse indicate that horses have become taller over the last 60 million years, as shown in the following table.

Time (millions of years ago)	Height (metres)
60	0.4
30	0.6
15	1.0
1 to the present	1.6

Genetic Engineering 17

Learning objectives

In this chapter you will learn about:

1 Genetic engineering
2 The process of genetic engineering
3 Applications of genetic engineering

Genetic engineering

Genetic engineering is the artificial alteration or manipulation of genes.

The process of genetic engineering involves removing a gene (called the target gene) from one organism and inserting it into the DNA of another organism. In this respect it is really a 'cut and paste' process.

The altered DNA is called recombinant DNA. The organism that contains the recombinant DNA is called a genetically modified organism (GMO).

If the DNA is transferred from one species to another, the organism that receives the DNA is said to be transgenic. Examples of genetic engineering include:

— A human gene inserted into a bacterium
— A human gene inserted into another animal
— A bacterial gene inserted into a plant.

Alternative names

Genetic engineering is also called genetic manipulation or modification, recombinant DNA technology, gene splicing, and gene cloning.

The process of genetic engineering

The following example will explain how a human gene (such as the gene for insulin production) is inserted into a bacterium so that the bacterium can produce human insulin.

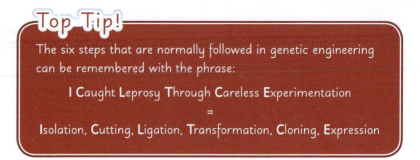
Isolation

Isolation involves the removal (or isolation) of the human DNA (or chromosome) and the bacterial DNA (which is usually a loop of DNA called a plasmid) from their cells. Plasmids carry genes for antibiotic resistance.

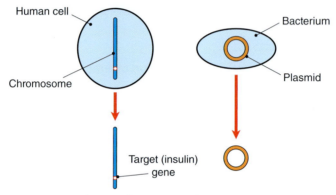

Isolation of human and bacterial DNA

Cutting

Both the human and bacterial DNA are cut using the same type of enzyme.

The enzyme is called a **restriction enzyme** because it is restricted to cutting DNA at a specific base sequence. The cut sections of human DNA are mixed with the opened bacterial plasmid. This allows the human DNA to be inserted into the plasmid.

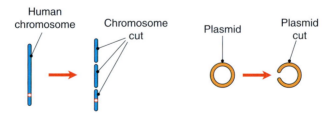

Ligation

Ligation **is the process by which the exposed ends of the human DNA and the plasmid DNA are joined or spliced together.** Ligation is carried out using a special enzyme called DNA ligase. The objective is for the target gene to combine with a plasmid. In reality most of the combinations involve a plasmid joining with another plasmid or a plasmid joining with one or more sections of human DNA that do not contain the target gene.

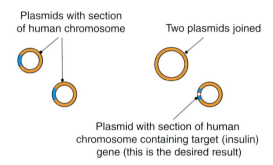

Plasmids with section of human chromosome

Two plasmids joined

Plasmid with section of human chromosome containing target (insulin) gene (this is the desired result)

Transformation

Transformation **is the uptake of DNA into a cell.** Normally the bacterial cells are specially treated to enable them to take in plasmids. Only a few of the bacterial cells take in a plasmid. Even then, many of the plasmids do not contain a copy of the target gene.

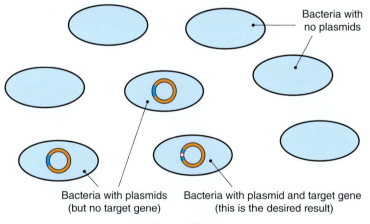

Bacteria with no plasmids

Bacteria with plasmids (but no target gene)

Bacteria with plasmid and target gene (this is the desired result)

Cutting and ligation

Cloning

Growing the bacterial cells on agar containing an antibiotic identifies the cells that contain plasmids. Only the bacterial cells that contain a plasmid can grow (because of the antibiotic resistance gene on the plasmid). As the bacteria reproduce, so do the number of plasmids. The plasmids are used to make multiple copies of the target gene. The plasmids are said to be **cloning vectors**.

Many colonies (clusters) of bacteria grow on the agar. Only some of these colonies contain plasmids with the target gene. These colonies are identified using radioactive probes, which are sections of DNA that are complementary to the target gene.

Once the bacteria that contain the target gene are identified, they are removed and cloned (grown) on fresh agar.

Expression

Expression **is the production of the desired product from the GMO (in this case the bacteria).** The bacteria with the target gene are grown in bioreactors with the correct nutrients, pH, temperature, etc., and allowed to form the product (such as insulin). This is an example of biotechnology.

The product is isolated from the liquid and bacteria in the bioreactor (this often involves difficult filtrations). The product is then purified for distribution.

Applications of genetic engineering

Plant	Animal	Micro-organism
Many commercially grown plants have been genetically engineered so they contain **bacterial** genes. These genes make the plants resistant to certain weedkiller (or herbicide) sprays. This means that the weedkiller kills weeds but does not affect the genetically modified crop.	A **human** gene has been inserted into a sheep's zygote. This allows the adult sheep to produce a clotting chemical needed by haemophiliacs to clot their blood.	The **human** insulin gene has been inserted into a bacterium. This allows the bacteria to produce insulin for use by diabetics.

The Five Kingdoms

18

The five kingdoms

Living things are divided into five kingdoms:

- Monera
- Protoctista (Protists)
- Fungi
- Plants
- Animals

Monera

Example: bacteria

Features

- Absence of a membrane-enclosed nucleus (therefore they are prokaryotes)
- Absence of membrane-enclosed organelles (such as mitochondria and chloroplasts)
- Normally small and single-celled
- Usually reproduce asexually.

Protoctista (Protists)

Examples: algae (including seaweeds and plankton), amoeba

Features

- Have a membrane-enclosed nucleus (therefore they are eukaryotic)
- Mostly single-celled or simple multi-celled organisms
- Mainly found in water.

Fungi

Examples: mushrooms, moulds, mildew, yeast, rhizopus

Features

- Heterotrophic (take in their food)
- Mainly multi-celled with tubes called hyphae
- Hyphae walls are made of chitin (a carbohydrate)
- Mainly reproduce by spores.

Plants

Examples: mosses, ferns, pine trees, grasses, flowering plants

Features

- Complex multi-celled organisms
- Autotrophic (make their own food by photosynthesis)
- Cell walls made of cellulose
- Cells contain large vacuoles
- Non-motile
- Reproduce sexually and asexually
- Embryo is protected inside parent plant.

Animals

Examples: sponges, jellyfish, flatworms, roundworms, segmented worms, snails, insects (all invertebrates), fish, frogs, snakes, birds and humans (all vertebrates)

Features

- Multi-celled
- Heterotrophic (take in food)
- Absence of cell walls
- Presence of nervous and muscular systems (to allow rapid movements)
- Normally reproduce sexually
- Large non-motile egg and small motile sperm (with a tail or flagellum).

Monera

19

Learning objectives

In this chapter you will learn about:

1 Structure of a typical bacterium
2 Types of bacteria
3 Reproduction
4 Endospores
5 Conditions for bacterial growth
6 Growth curve
7 Food processing
8 Beneficial and harmful bacteria
9 Antibiotics

Structure of a typical bacterium

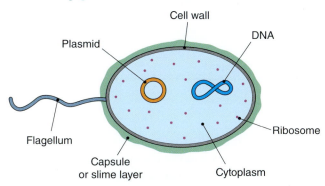

Function of the cell parts of a bacterium

Part	Function
Capsule/slime layer	The capsule is a dry layer while the slime layer is moist. Both serve to prevent water loss.
Cell wall	The cell wall protects and prevents the cell from expanding and bursting.
Flagellum	The flagellum (plural: flagella) allows the cell to move or swim. Only found in some bacteria.

Cell membrane	The cell membrane retains the cell contents and controls what passes in and out of the cell.
DNA	The loop of DNA contains the genes that control the cell.
Plasmid	The plasmid is a small loop of DNA that contains genes (which may control antibiotic resistance, for example).
Ribosome	The ribosome makes protein.

Types of bacteria

Bacteria are classified according to their shape into rod-, round- and spiral-shaped.

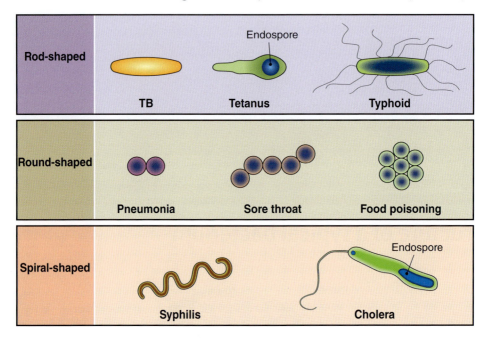

Reproduction

Bacterial reproduction is asexual. The method of reproduction is called binary fission. The loop of DNA replicates and the identical loops of DNA move to each end of the cell. The cell membrane and cell wall pinch in to form two cells, each containing a loop of DNA with identical genes.

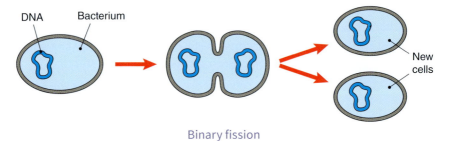

Binary fission

Under ideal conditions bacteria reproduce every 20 minutes. This means that they double in number every 20 minutes. The short life cycle means that mutations (such as resistance to an antibiotic) spread very fast from generation to generation in bacteria.

Endospores

When conditions are unfavourable the bacterial DNA replicates, and a tough, resistant wall forms around one of the DNA loops inside the existing cell. The resulting endospore can survive unfavourable conditions.

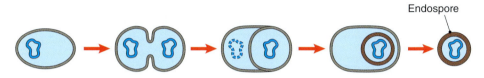

Endospore

When conditions are favourable the endospore absorbs water, and the cell grows and reproduces by binary fission.

Conditions for bacterial growth

Nutrition

Bacteria may be autotrophic or heterotrophic.

Autotrophic **means that an organism makes its own food.**

Heterotrophic **means that an organism takes in food.**

Autotrophic bacteria

Autotrophic bacteria may be photosynthetic or chemosynthetic.

- **Photosynthetic** bacteria make food using light energy, e.g. purple sulfur bacteria.
- **Chemosynthetic** bacteria make food by converting one chemical into another, e.g. nitrifying bacteria in the soil, which convert nitrogen compounds into nitrates.

Heterotrophic bacteria

Heterotrophic bacteria may be saprophytic or parasitic.

- *Saprophytes* **live on and take in food from dead sources.** Bacteria of decay are examples of saprophytic bacteria.
- *Parasites* **take in food from a live host and usually harm the host.** Disease-causing bacteria such as pneumonia, tetanus and typhoid are examples of parasitic bacteria.

Temperature

Temperature affects the rate of bacterial action by influencing the rate of enzyme action. Most bacteria prefer a temperature between 20 and 30°C, but disease-causing bacteria prefer a temperature of 37°C.

Oxygen concentration

Aerobic bacteria **need oxygen for respiration.** ***Anaerobic bacteria*** **do not require oxygen for respiration.**

Obligate aerobes must have oxygen for respiration (i.e. they are obliged to have oxygen).

Facultative aerobes can respire with or without using oxygen (i.e. they have the facility to use or not to use oxygen).

pH

Bacterial enzymes work at specific pH values. Outside the optimum pH range the bacterial enzymes are denatured. Most bacteria work most efficiently at pH 7.

External solute concentration

- If the environment outside a bacterial cell has a **lower solute concentration** than the bacterium, water will pass into the bacterium by osmosis. Most bacteria live in these conditions. The cell wall prevents the bacterium from expanding and bursting.

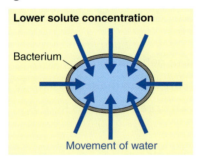

- If the environment outside a bacterial cell has a **higher solute concentration** than the bacterium, water will pass out of the bacterium by osmosis. The bacterium will not be able to grow and reproduce due to a shortage of water.

  This is the basis of preserving food by salting (e.g. fish) and high sugar concentrations (e.g. jams).

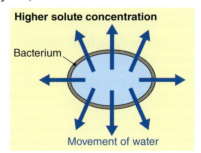

Pressure

High pressure damages bacterial cell walls. To allow bacteria to survive in bioreactors that require high pressure, genetically modified bacteria are used.

Growth curve

The changes in the number of bacteria growing on a limited food supply (such as on agar in a petri dish) are represented by the following graph.

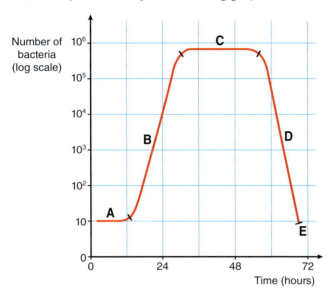

Note that the number of bacteria is shown on a log (or exponential) scale. This is to allow for the large number of bacteria that are formed. The graph can be analysed under five separate phases.

Phase	Bacterial numbers	Reason
The lag phase (A)	The number of bacteria does not change.	The bacteria are making the correct enzymes to digest the substrate they are on.
The log phase (B)	The number of bacteria increases rapidly.	The growth conditions are ideal and the bacterial numbers double every 20 minutes.
The stationary phase (C)	The number of bacteria does not change (it may even fall slightly).	Growth conditions are no longer ideal. The bacteria may be short of food, water, space or oxygen or their own toxic products may inhibit reproduction.
The decline phase (D)	The number of bacteria falls rapidly.	This happens for the same reasons given for the stationary phase.
The survival phase (E)	A small number of bacteria may survive.	The bacteria remain dormant as spores.

Food processing

Modern bioprocessing uses bacteria (and other organisms such as yeasts) to produce a wide range of food products. These products include yoghurt, cheeses, sweeteners, amino acids, flavourings, taste enhancers, vitamins, protein foods such as single-cell protein (SCP) and alcohol.

There are two main methods of food processing: batch and continuous flow.

Batch food processing

- In batch processing a bioreactor is sterilised. A batch of nutrients is added to a small sample of the micro-organism in the bioreactor. The correct temperature, pressure, pH, gases and other relevant conditions are applied.
- The bioreactor is closed.
- The micro-organisms go through the lag, log and stationary phases of the standard growth curve. The product is formed at the log and stationary phases.
- The process is often stopped before the decline phase in order to prevent the micro-organisms from dying, bursting or producing unwanted side products (although antibiotics are formed during the decline phase).
- The product is removed from the bioreactor, separated from the micro-organisms and purified.
- The bioreactor is sterilised and the process starts again.

Advantages

- It is a simple process.
- It allows small volumes of product to form.
- The micro-organisms grow well (naturally).

Continuous-flow food processing

- In continuous-flow food processing, nutrients are added to the bioreactor at the same rate at which the product is withdrawn. The conditions in the bioreactor are controlled as normal.
- The bioreactor is left open for the inflow of nutrients and the outflow of the product.
- The micro-organisms are kept at the log phase of growth. This allows them to produce their product in great quantities over long periods of time.

Advantages

- Production is continuous (no time is wasted).
- There is no need to sterilise the bioreactor so often.
- Product is formed more rapidly (as the micro-organisms are very active in the log phase).

Beneficial and harmful bacteria

Beneficial	Harmful
Make yoghurt and cheese	Cause food to decay
Genetically engineered bacteria make enzymes and hormones.	Pathogenic bacteria cause diseases such as pneumonia and tetanus.

Antibiotics

Antibiotics **are chemicals produced by bacteria and fungi that kill or prevent the growth of bacteria.**

Antibiotics have no effect on viruses. Examples of antibiotics are penicillin and streptomycin.

Antibiotic resistance

- When an antibiotic is first used, it kills all the bacteria in an organism. Sooner or later a mutation in one bacterium will cause that bacterium to be resistant to the antibiotic. The gene for antibiotic resistance is usually found on the bacterial plasmid.
- As all the antibiotic-sensitive bacteria are killed off, the resistant bacterium has no competition and can form huge numbers of resistant bacteria. This resistance can be passed to other bacteria by transferring copies of the plasmid to the other bacteria.
- In this way bacteria have developed resistance to most (and in some cases all) known antibiotics. These bacteria are called multi-resistant bacteria.
- The over-use of antibiotics (in animal feeds, by doctors prescribing antibiotics when they are not absolutely necessary and by patients not completing the prescribed dose) has accelerated the evolution of multi-resistant bacteria.

20 Fungi

Learning objectives

In this chapter you will learn about:

1 Types of fungi
2 *Rhizopus*
3 Yeast
4 Laboratory procedures for handling micro-organisms
5 Beneficial and harmful fungi

Types of fungi

Fungi may be parasitic/saprophytic and edible/non-edible.

Parasitic fungi

Parasitic fungi take their food from **living things**. They mostly feed off plants (e.g. potato blight fungus) and cause diseases such as smuts, rusts and mildews.

Athlete's foot and ringworm are examples of parasitic fungi that affect humans.

Saprophytic fungi

Saprophytic fungi take their food from **dead sources**. These fungi feed off dead plants and animals and cause decay. Examples include mushrooms and moulds.

Edible fungi

Some fungi (such as field mushrooms and morels) are safe to eat.

Poisonous fungi

Some fungi are poisonous (such as the death cap and destroying angels, both in the genus *Amanita*). It is not easy to distinguish between an edible and a poisonous fungus.

Rhizopus

Rhizopus (also called black bread mould or common bread mould) is a fungus that grows on bread and other starchy food. Its mode of nutrition is heterotrophic (or saprophytic).

Structure of *Rhizopus*

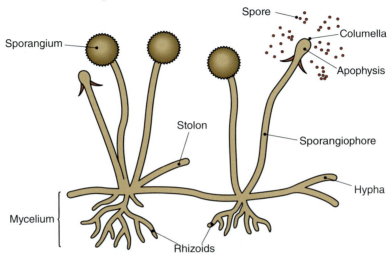

Structure of a rhizopus

Part	Description or function
Hypha	A hypha is a tube. Each hypha secretes enzymes into the substrate and absorbs the digested material.
Mycelium	A mycelium is a mass of hyphae.
Stolon	A stolon is a hypha that grows over the surface of the food to allow a new mycelium to develop.
Rhizoids	Rhizoids create a larger surface area for the absorption of food.
Sporangiophore	The sporangiophore supports the sporangium and allows the spores to be more easily dispersed.

Reproduction

Asexual reproduction: This is carried out by both the stolons and spores, though mainly the latter, which are dispersed by the air.

Sexual reproduction: Sexual reproduction in *Rhizopus* is a method of survival (i.e. it is not a method of increasing the number or amount of the fungus). It takes place when two strains of the fungus grow close together.

Events in sexual reproduction

- Two hyphae grow close together.
- Swellings develop on each hypha.
- Nuclei, which are the sex cells or gametes, move into each swelling.
- Each swelling is now called a progametangium.
- A wall forms behind the nuclei.
- The swellings (now called gametangia) touch.
- The end walls between the gametangia break down.
- Fertilisation occurs when two haploid (n) nuclei join.
- A diploid (2n) zygote is formed.
- A tough wall forms around each zygote to produce a zygospore.
- The parent hyphae die.
- The zygospore remains dormant.
- When conditions are suitable, the diploid zygospore grows, by meiosis, to form a new haploid hypha.
- The new hypha soon forms a sporangium and the spores are dispersed.

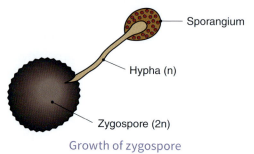

Growth of zygospore

Yeast

Structure

Yeast is a unicellular fungus which respires anaerobically according to the equation:

Glucose → 2 ethanol + 2 carbon dioxide

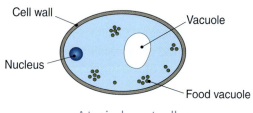

A typical yeast cell

Reproduction

Reproduction in yeast is asexual and is called **budding**.

The nucleus divides by mitosis. One of the daughter nuclei moves into the bud, which then detaches from the parent cell.

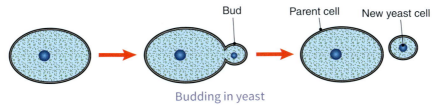

Budding in yeast

Laboratory procedures for handling micro-organisms

Sterile **means the absence of all living things.**

Sterilisation may be carried out in the following ways.

- Heat all equipment and materials to 120°C for 15 minutes in a pressure cooker or in an autoclave.
- Flame the tips of inoculating loops, forceps and the neck of any glassware by placing them briefly in a Bunsen flame.
- Soak all equipment in sterilising fluid (e.g. Milton) before disposing of it after use.

Asepsis **means that precautions are taken to prevent unwanted micro-organisms from contaminating the activity.**

Aseptic techniques involve some or all of the following.

- Wash your hands before and after handling all micro-organisms.
- Wash the bench with disinfectant.
- Keep all containers closed where possible.
- Open a container:
  - for the shortest possible time
  - the least possible distance.
- Seal any dish containing micro-organisms with tape.

Experiment

To investigate the growth of leaf yeasts

1. Cut some leaves from plants such as privet, ash or sycamore.
2. Wash your hands.
3. Disinfect the surface of the bench.
4. Place a blob of Vaseline on the upper surfaces of a number of the leaves. If necessary the leaves can be cut into small sections to fit into the petri dish. *(The Vaseline is used to attach the leaf to the inside cover of a petri dish.)*

5   Place the tips of a forceps in a Bunsen flame. *(This will sterilise them.)*

6   Barely open a petri dish containing sterile nutrient agar. *(Agar provides a solid medium; nutrient agar has food that allows micro-organisms to grow.)*

7   Use the flamed forceps to attach the Vaseline-covered surface of the leaf to the lid of the petri dish.

8   Place the lid on the petri dish.

9   Re-flame the tips of the forceps.

10   Seal the petri dish closed using tape or parafilm.

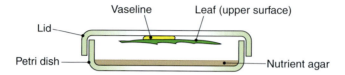

11   Seal a petri dish containing nutrient agar without adding a leaf. *(This acts as the control.)*

12   Label the petri dishes with a marker on the undersurface of the dish. *(This allows you to see through the top of the dish.)*

13   Leave the petri dishes upside down in a warm place (a laboratory will do, but an incubator at 25°C is better). *(If the dishes are upside down, condensation does not form on the inside of the lid.)*

14   After 3–4 days pink colonies (circles) of yeast are seen on the agar with the leaf. The control dish should not have any growth in it.

15   Sterilise all material (by covering the surface with disinfectant or Milton) before disposing of it. *(This is a safety precaution which prevents spores from being dispersed.)*

Note that yeasts are inhibited by air pollution. By comparing the growth of leaf yeasts on leaves from different environments the amount of air pollution may be indicated.

Beneficial and harmful fungi

Beneficial	Harmful
Yeast produces ethanol (beer and wine).	Fungi cause decay of crops, foods, paper and timber.
Some fungi are edible.	Some fungi cause plant and animal diseases.

Amoeba

21

Amoeba

- *Amoeba* is a single-celled organism. Each cell is about 0.1 mm in diameter and is more or less colourless.
- *Amoeba* is in the kingdom Protoctista, or Protista.
- *Amoeba* lives in fresh water and is heterotrophic, i.e. it feeds by eating other protists, plankton and animals.

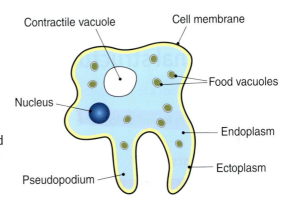

The structure of *Amoeba*

Functions of the parts

Part	Description or function
Cell membrane	Allows gas exchange and retains the cell contents
Nucleus	Surrounded by a membrane; it controls the cell
Contractile vacuole	Collects and eliminates water that enters the cell by osmosis; carries out osmoregulation
Pseupods (or pseudopodia)	These are false feet used for movement and feeding
Ectoplasm	The outer cytoplasm
Endoplasm	The inner cytoplasm
Food vacuoles	Digest the organisms that are taken in and pass nutrients into the cell

Shoot system

The shoot system is the part of the plant above ground level. It consists of the stem, leaves, flowers, seeds and fruits. Flowers, seeds and fruits will be studied in Chapter 38.

Function of stems

- To support the aerial parts of the plant
- To transport materials between the leaves and roots
- To store food.

Top Tip!

Phloem (containing the letter **o**) is on the **o**utside of the stem.

Transverse section (TS) of a stem

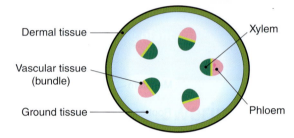

Dermal tissue

Vascular tissue (bundle)

Ground tissue

Xylem

Phloem

Transverse section (TS) of a stem

Longitudinal section (LS) of a stem

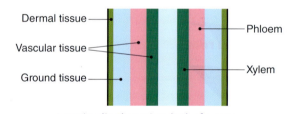

Dermal tissue

Vascular tissue

Ground tissue

Phloem

Xylem

Longitudinal section (LS) of a stem

Leaf

Function of leaves

- To carry out photosynthesis
- To exchange gases
- To allow water to pass out (transpiration)
- To store food.

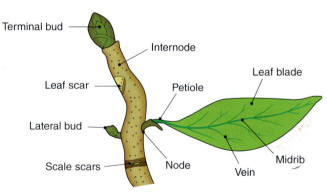

Terminal bud

Internode

Leaf scar

Petiole

Leaf blade

Lateral bud

Scale scars

Node

Vein

Midrib

External structure of leaf

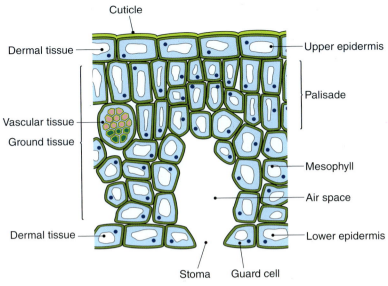

Cuticle

Dermal tissue — Upper epidermis

Palisade

Vascular tissue

Ground tissue

Mesophyll

Air space

Dermal tissue — Lower epidermis

Stoma   Guard cell

Internal structure of leaf

Classification of flowering plants

There are two major categories of flowering plants: monocotyledonous plants (monocots) and dicotyledonous plants (dicots). The main differences between monocots and dicots are given on the following table.

Monocots	Dicots
Seeds contain **one** cotyledon (which is a food store or seed leaf)	Seeds contain **two** cotyledons, or seed leaves
Mainly herbaceous (do not have woody parts)	Herbaceous or woody
Long narrow leaves	Broad leaves
Parallel veins in the leaf	The veins form a branching network
Vascular bundles are scattered at random in the stem	Vascular bundles form a ring in the stem
The flowering parts are in groups (or multiples) of three	The flowering parts are in groups (or multiples) of four or five
Examples include daffodils, tulips, grasses and cereals	Examples include beans, peas, busy lizzies, oak, elm and ash

To prepare and examine microscopically a transverse section (TS) of a dicot stem

1 Use a wet-backed blade or a scalpel to cut thin sections of a herbaceous stem (such as a busy lizzie). *(The sections should be thin so that light can pass through them when viewed under a microscope. If the blade is wet it cuts more smoothly through the plant tissues. The backed blade is used for safety.)*

2 Cut away from your hand *(to avoid cutting yourself)*.

3 Store the sections in a petri dish or clock glass of water *(to prevent dehydration)*.

4 Transfer the sections using a small artist's paint brush.

5 Transfer the thinnest sections onto a microscope slide.

6 The sections may be stained (with iodine, for example).

7 Lower a cover slip at an angle on to the sections. *(This eliminate air bubbles. The cover slip protects the lens.)*

8 Observe under the microscope at a low power.

9 Move the slide so that any area of interest is centred. Then observe under the microscope at a high power.

10 Draw a diagram of the stem as you see it. Label the dermal, vascular and ground tissues on your diagram.

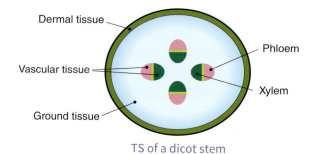

TS of a dicot stem

Transport, Storage and Gas Exchange in Flowering Plants 23

Water uptake by roots

- The solute concentration in root cells is higher than the solute concentration of the water in the soil.
- Water from the soil enters root hairs by osmosis. The root hairs have the following adaptations for absorbing water:
  — Large numbers
  — A large surface area
  — Thin walls that are fully permeable
  — Cell membranes that are semi-permeable
  — No cuticle.
- Water passes from cell to cell across the ground tissue (also called cortex) in the root until it enters xylem.
- Xylem forms a hollow pipeline that runs from the roots, through the stem and into the leaves.
- Water passes up through the xylem to the leaf.

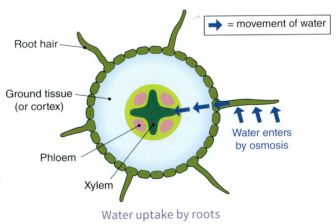

= movement of water

Root hair

Ground tissue (or cortex)

Phloem

Xylem

Water enters by osmosis

Water uptake by roots

Water rising through stems

Water rises up through the stem by two mechanisms: root pressure and cohesion–tension.

Root pressure

Root pressure is caused by the build-up of water in the root cells due to osmosis. This pressure forces water up through the xylem in a plant. Root pressure alone is not enough to push a column of water to the top of very high plants.

The cohesion–tension model

In 1894 Henry Dixon and John Joly in Trinity College Dublin first proposed this model for the movement of water in xylem.

- *Cohesion* **is the force of attraction between similar molecules.** Water has a high cohesion. This means that water molecules tend to stick together.

- *Adhesion* **is the force of attraction between different molecules.** The adhesive force between water and xylem walls is lower than the cohesive force between water molecules.

- The balance between the cohesive and adhesive forces means that if a column of water is pulled up in xylem, the water molecules tend to stick to each other rather than sticking to the walls of the xylem.

- *Transpiration* **is the loss of water vapour from a plant.** Most transpiration takes place when water molecules evaporate from the air spaces in a leaf out through openings called **stomata**. The cells in the leaf become less turgid and water moves out of the xylem by osmosis. Transpiration may also occur through openings in the stem called **lenticels**.

- When water moves out of the xylem, this pulls up the water molecules in the rest of the xylem due to cohesion. The pull creates a **tension** in the column of water.

- To prevent them from collapsing inwards under the upward pressure, xylem is strengthened with **lignin**.

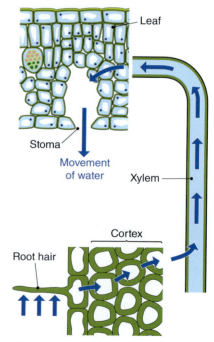

The movement of water in a plant

Control of transpiration in leaves

The flow of water through a plant is called the transpiration stream.

To reduce the rate of transpiration (and prevent the plant from wilting and dying) leaves have the following features.

Waxy cuticle

The cuticle is a waterproof layer located mainly on the upper epidermis of a leaf. It reduces transpiration.

Stomatal opening and closing

Each stoma (plural: stomata) is surrounded by two guard cells. The guard cells can change shape to open or close the stoma. The stomata open to allow gas exchange and close to prevent excess water loss.

Mineral and carbon dioxide uptake and transport

Minerals

Minerals such as calcium and magnesium are absorbed by the roots in the form of ions (charged particles). Minerals are absorbed by a combination of **diffusion** (which is passive) and **active transport** (which requires energy). Minerals are transported around the plant dissolved in water in the xylem.

Carbon dioxide

Carbon dioxide is necessary for photosynthesis. Some of the CO_2 enters the leaf by **diffusion** when the stomata are open. However, the leaf can also use CO_2 that is released by the mitochondria in **respiration**.

Control of stomatal opening

The controlling factor in the opening and closing of the stomata is carbon dioxide concentration. The guard cells have extra thick walls on the sides that touch each other. When the plant is carrying out photosynthesis, CO_2 is absorbed by the chloroplasts. The low concentration of CO_2 causes water to **enter** the guard cells by osmosis (the exact reason why this happens is still unknown). The guard cells swell. Due to their irregular cell walls they form a kidney shape. This causes the stoma to open.

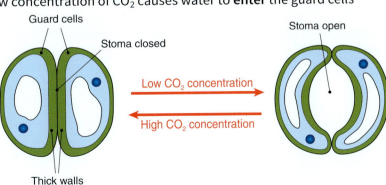

Stomatal opening and closing

When the CO_2 concentration is high (e.g. when CO_2 is not being used in photosynthesis) the guard cells **lose** water by osmosis. The cells become smaller and the stoma closes.

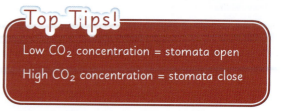

Top Tips!

Low CO_2 concentration = stomata open

High CO_2 concentration = stomata close

The products of photosynthesis

The initial products of photosynthesis are glucose and oxygen.

Sometimes these products are used in the leaf.

- Glucose may be used for respiration, stored in the leaf as starch or converted to cellulose for cell walls.
- Some of the oxygen in the leaf is used for respiration.

Very often the products of photosynthesis move out of the leaf.

- Glucose is converted to sucrose and transported around the plant in phloem. The transport of food in phloem is called **translocation**.
- Sucrose may be converted to starch for storage in other parts of the plant.
- Oxygen may diffuse out of the leaf into the air.

Plant food-storage organs

Plant food-storage organs include altered or modified roots, stems and leaves.

Modified roots

In dicots the first root from the seed grows to form a tap root. Tap roots often swell with stored food, e.g. carrots, sugar beet, parsnips and turnips.

Modified stems

Some plants have an underground stem system. The tips of these stems swell to store food in structures called tubers. An example of a stem tuber is the potato.

Modified leaves

Plants such as onions and daffodils produce modified underground leaves called bulbs.

Cabbage and lettuce also have leaves that store food. Rhubarb and celery have petioles modified to store food.

Blood

24

Learning objectives

In this chapter you will learn about:

1 Composition of blood

2 The functions of blood

3 Blood groups

Composition of blood

Blood is composed of four parts: plasma, red blood cells, white blood cells and platelets.

Plasma

- Plasma is the liquid part of blood.
- Plasma is a pale yellow liquid and makes up about 55% of the blood.
- Plasma is composed of:
  — 90% water
  — 7% protein
  — 3% dissolved materials.
- The main proteins in plasma are:
  — Antibodies (which fight infection)
  — Clotting proteins.

Function

Plasma transports useful materials such as glucose, amino acids, vitamins and hormones, along with wastes such as salts, urea and carbon dioxide. Plasma also transports heat around the body.

If the clotting proteins are removed from plasma, the resulting liquid is called serum.

Red blood cells

Red blood cells are made in the bone marrow of long bones such as the ribs, breastbone, and the long bones in the arms and legs. Each red blood cell has a nucleus when it is first formed; this dies within a few days. Red blood cells do not have a nucleus or mitochondria and consist of a membrane that surrounds an iron-containing protein called haemoglobin.

Function

Red blood cells transport oxygen. To allow them to absorb as much oxygen as possible the cells are a biconcave shape (see below).

$$\text{Haemoglobin} + O_2 \quad \rightarrow \quad \text{Oxyhaemoglobin}$$
$$\text{(purple)} \qquad\qquad\qquad \text{(bright red)}$$

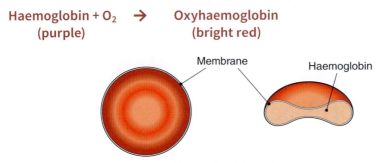

Shape of red blood cells

Red blood cells cannot repair themselves. As a result they live for only about 4 months.

Dead red blood cells are broken down in the spleen and liver.

- The iron is retained to be recycled into new haemoglobin.
- The rest of the cell is converted into bile pigments.

White blood cells

- Are colourless
- Are about twice the size of red cells
- Have a nucleus and mitochondria
- Have no definite shape
- Live for a few days
- Can reproduce themselves
- Are less numerous than red cells (1:700).

White blood cells are formed in bone marrow and some of them mature in the lymphatic system.

Function

White blood cells defend the body against infection by engulfing pathogens and by producing antibodies.

Lymphocytes

Lymphocytes make up 25% of white blood cells. They are stored in parts of the lymphatic system. They contain large, rounded nuclei that almost fill the entire cell.

Function

The main function of lymphocytes is to make antibodies. Antibodies are proteins that destroy foreign cells in the body.

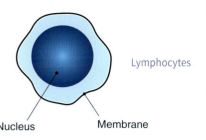

Lymphocytes

Nucleus   Membrane

Monocytes

Monocytes make up 5% of white blood cells. They are the largest type of white blood cell. They normally have a large, kidney-shaped nucleus.

Function

Monocytes surround and engulf pathogens such as bacteria and viruses. The way in which they do this is called phagocytosis. Monocytes are often called phagocytes or macrophages.

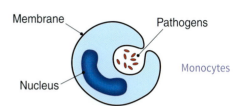

Membrane   Pathogens

Monocytes

Nucleus

Platelets

Platelets are made in bone marrow. A large cell, called a megacyte, is formed and then splits into fragments. These fragments are the platelets.

Platelets have no nuclei and are not cells (but they are made from cells).

Top Tip!

Although there are many types of white blood cell, only lymphocytes and monocytes are on the course.

Function

- Platelets allow blood to clot.
- Blood clots:
  - Prevent blood loss
  - Prevent the entry of foreign cells into the body.

The functions of blood

Transport

- Food, salts, carbon dioxide, urea and hormones in plasma
- Oxygen in red blood cells
- Heat in plasma

Fight infection

- White blood cells (monocytes) surround and destroy pathogens
- White blood cells (lymphocytes) make antibodies which destroy pathogens
- Platelets clot blood, which prevents the entry of pathogens

Blood groups

ABO groups

Red blood cells may have different chemicals (called antigens) on the outer surface of their membranes. The main two antigens that may be on a red blood cell are called A and B.

Depending on the type of antigen present (if any), red blood cells are assigned to one of four blood groups: A, B, AB and O.

Blood group	Antigen on red blood cell
A	A
B	B
AB	A and B
O	None

Rhesus factor

Apart from antigens A and B, some red blood cells may have another antigen on their surface called the Rhesus factor or antigen D.

- Cells that have the Rhesus antigen are Rhesus positive or simply positive (+).
- Cells that do not have the Rhesus antigen are Rhesus negative or simply negative (–).

Example of blood group	Antigen
AB+	A and B and Rhesus factor
A–	A (but no Rhesus factor)
O+	Rhesus factor

Importance of blood groups

Blood groups are very important when receiving blood transfusions. If blood groups are mixed incorrectly, antibodies in the person receiving the blood will react with antigens in the donated blood. This will cause blood to clump and may result in death.

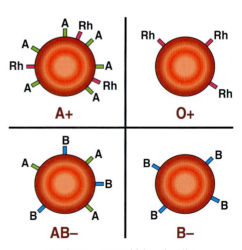

Antigens on red blood cells

The Human Defence System

Pathogens

A *pathogen* is a foreign body or cell that causes disease.

Pathogens include bacteria, viruses and fungi. Humans defend themselves against pathogens using two defence systems: the general defence system and the specific defence system.

The general defence system

The *general* defence system tries to defend us against all pathogens.

The general defence system acts by preventing the entry of pathogens into the body or by destroying them when they do enter.

Preventing entry

- **Skin** acts as a barrier to the entry of pathogens.
- **Lysozyme** is an enzyme that is found in sweat, tears, saliva and urine. It bursts the walls of bacteria, leading to their death.
- **Clotting** helps to prevent the entry of pathogens once our skin is damaged.
- **Mucus** in the respiratory system is sticky. It traps pathogens.
- **Cilia** in the respiratory system sweep the mucus up from the air passages. The mucus (and the pathogens) then passes to the stomach.
- **Acid** in the stomach (hydrochloric acid) destroys pathogens. Lactic acid in the vagina acts in the same way.

Destroying pathogens in the body

- **White blood cells** surround and destroy pathogens that enter the body. These cells are often called phagocytes. Large phagocytes are called macrophages.

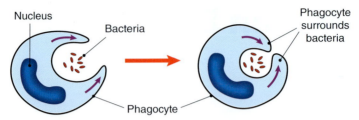

The action of phagocytes

- **Complement** is a set of proteins found in the plasma. Complement is activated by infection and causes bacterial cell walls to burst.
- **Interferons** are another set of proteins. They are produced by body cells that become infected by viruses. Interferons prevent (interfere with) the multiplication of viruses.
- **Inflammation** results in heat, redness and swelling around the site of infection. This increases the number of white blood cells in the area of infection. If the inflammation occurs all over the body it is called a fever.

The specific defence system (the immune system)

The specific defence (or immune) system **acts against one type of pathogen or antigen.**

Antigens/antibodies

An *antigen* is a foreign substance that stimulates the production of antibodies.

Antigens:

- Are **anti**body-**gen**erating molecules
- Are found on the surface of pathogens such as viruses and bacteria
- Are also associated with pollen grains, blood transfusions, transplants and cancer cells.

An *antibody* is a protein produced by white blood cells in response to an antigen.

Antibody production

- Monocytes recognise antigens on the surface of pathogens.
- Monocytes surround and digest the pathogens.
- Once digested, the monocytes display the antigens on their outer surface.

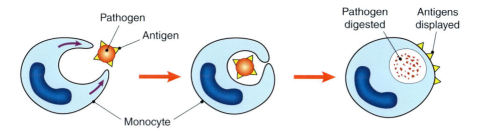

- The antigens then stimulate other white blood cells, called lymphocytes, to multiply and produce huge amounts of the correct antibody to react with the antigen.
- There is a very exact fit between the antibody and the antigen.
- Each antibody will fit only one specific antigen.

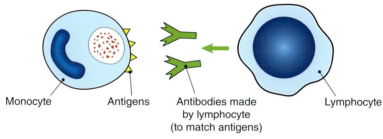

Monocyte   Antigens   Antibodies made   Lymphocyte
                                by lymphocyte
                                (to match antigens)

Antibody production

Antibody action

Antibodies inactivate antigens in the following ways.

- They prevent the bacteria and viruses (which carry the antigens) from entering cells. This allows phagocytes to destroy them.
- They cause the antigen-containing cells to clump, which allows phagocytes to destroy them.
- They trigger the complement system that causes the pathogen cells to burst.

Duration of Immunity

Once an infection is overcome, some of the lymphocytes that made the antibodies will live in the body for many years. If the same antigen enters the body again these lymphocytes will multiply and produce the correct antibody. This means we have **permanent immunity** from the specific antigen. We can get a cold or flu more than once because there is more than one type of cold and flu. Each type has a differently shaped antigen that requires a different antibody to counteract it.

On second or subsequent infection antibodies are produced:

- In response to much smaller amounts of the antigen
- More quickly (in 5 rather than 14 days)
- In much greater numbers.

The features and types of B-cell and T-cell

Lymphocytes are one type of white blood cell. All lymphocytes are formed in the bone marrow. Depending on where they mature, lymphocytes are divided into two main groups: B-lymphocytes (B-cells) and T-lymphocytes (T-cells).

B-cells

- B-cells are made in bone marrow and mature in the bone marrow.
- Once they are mature B-cells move to the lymph nodes.
- B-cells produce antibodies.
- Humans are born with millions of different B-cells.
- Each B-cell produces one specifically shaped antibody.
- If their antibodies fit an antigen, the B-cell multiplies (forms a clone) and starts to produce large amounts of the antibody.
- Most of the B-cells die once the infection is overcome. However, a small number live on as memory cells. These cells ensure that we do not suffer from the same infection more than once.

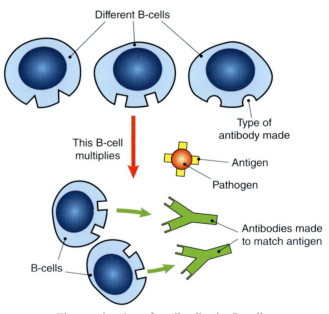

The production of antibodies by B-cells

T-cells

- T-cells are made in bone marrow but mature and are activated in the thymus gland.
- The thymus gland is in the chest.
- T-cells do not produce antibodies.

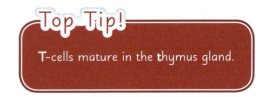

There are four different types of T-cell.

1 **Helper T-cells** recognise antigens on monocytes.

   — Helper T-cells produce chemicals that stimulate the correct B-cells to multiply. The B-cells then make the correct antibody.

   — Helper T-cells also stimulate the production of killer T-cells.

2 **Killer T-cells** attack and destroy abnormal body cells.

   — Abnormal body cells include cells infected with viruses and cancer cells.

   — Killer T-cells are also called natural killer (NK) cells. They are said to be cytotoxic, i.e. they kill cells.

3 **Suppressor T-cells** inhibit B-cells and killer T-cells.

   — Suppressor T-cells are stimulated to multiply by the presence of specific antigens.

   — They grow slowly and normally become active after the pathogens have been destroyed. In this way they turn off the immune response when the pathogens have been destroyed.

4 **Memory T-cells** stimulate B-cells and killer T-cells to multiply if the same antigen enters the body again.

   — After an infection memory T-cells live for many years, often for the life of the person.

   — They prevent the same pathogen (or antigen) from infecting the body a second time.

Induced immunity (active/passive, natural/artificial)

Induced immunity is the ability to produce antibodies against specific antigens.

Active induced immunity

Active induced immunity means that the body produces its own antibodies.

This gives long-term (permanent) immunity because memory cells survive in the body.

There are two types of active induced immunity: natural and artificial

1 **Natural** active induced immunity is the way in which the body responds to the entry of an antigen in the normal manner, i.e. it is the antigen/antibody reaction as outlined above.

2 **Artificial** active induced immunity involves injecting or ingesting small doses of non-reproductive antigen. This stimulates the production of antibodies without the person suffering from the infection. This method is often called vaccination or immunisation. Examples include treatment for diphtheria, TB (the BCG injection), polio, meningitis and MMR (measles, mumps and rubella). **A vaccine is a non-reproductive dose of an antigen designed to stimulate antibodies.**

Passive induced immunity

Passive induced immunity happens when antibodies pass from one organism to another (usually from the mother to her baby).

This gives short-term immunity because the antibodies last only about 6 months and no memory cells are produced.

There are two types of passive induced immunity: natural and artificial.

1 **Natural** passive induced immunity occurs when antibodies pass from a mother to her child. This may take place in the womb or when the mother breastfeeds the baby.

   Babies do not normally suffer from common infections for the first 6 months of their lives as they receive antibodies from their mother. Breastfeeding extends this period of immunity.

2 **Artificial** passive induced immunity occurs when antibodies are injected into a person to counteract a specific disease. A common example is the tetanus jab. Antibodies are given for fast-acting infections or when vaccines are not available.

The Heart and Blood Vessels 26

Learning objectives

In this chapter you will learn about:

1. The need for a circulatory system
2. Open and closed circulatory systems
3. The structure and functions of blood vessels
4. The structure of the heart
5. Double circulation
6. The stages of a heartbeat
7. How heartbeat is controlled
8. Human circulatory system
9. Blood pressure
10. Lifestyle and the heart

The need for a circulatory system

In small organisms diffusion is sufficient to allow molecules to move from one place to another. However, in large organisms diffusion is too slow. This means that larger organisms need some sort of circulatory system.

Open and closed circulatory systems

Open circulatory system

In an **open circulatory system**, blood is pumped by the heart into blood vessels. The blood then leaves these vessels and passes slowly through different parts of the body. It then rejoins blood vessels and is carried back to the heart.

Animals with open circulatory systems include insects, spiders and crabs.

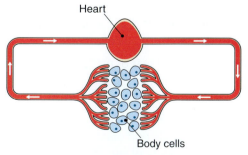

Open circulatory system

Closed circulatory system

In a closed circulatory system, blood is always enclosed in blood vessels. Humans have this type of system.

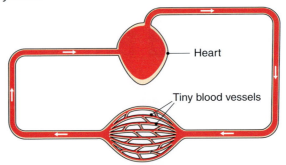

Closed circulatory system

The advantages of a closed circulatory system are:

- Blood can circulate faster round the body
- The flow of blood to different parts of the body is easier to regulate, e.g. when we are active we can direct more blood to our muscles.

The structure and function of blood vessels

Blood vessels

Arteries	Veins
Carry blood away from the heart	Carry blood to the heart
Blood is under high pressure	Blood is under low pressure
Thick, strong walls	Thin, weaker walls
Small lumen	Large lumen
No valves	Have valves

Structure of arteries and veins

Arteries and veins have similar structures. The main difference is that the walls of a vein are thinner than the walls of an artery.

- The outer layer of protein, called collagen, is a tough layer that prevents the vessel from expanding too much.
- The muscle and elastic fibres can alter the size of the vessel.
- The endothelium is a thin layer of living cells.

Top Tip!

A is for Arteries, which carry blood Away from the heart.

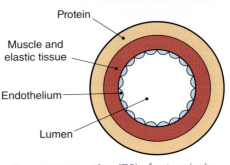

Transverse section (TS) of artery/vein

Valves

The blood pressure in veins is lower than it is in arteries. There is, therefore, a danger that the blood in a vein might flow backwards (i.e. away from the heart). To prevent this, veins have valves.

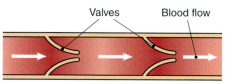

Valves in a vein

Capillaries

Capillaries are tiny, much-branched blood vessels. They have very thin walls (only one cell thick) that are porous. This means that materials can easily pass in and out of capillaries.

The function of capillaries is to allow exchange of materials between the blood and the cells of the body.

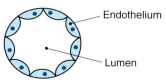

TS of a capillary

The structure of the heart

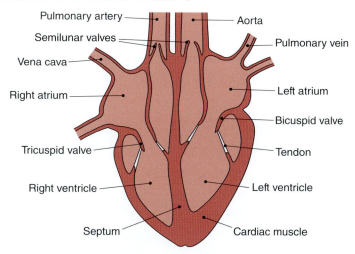

Structure of the heart

Blood flow through the heart

Deoxygenated blood (coming from all over the body) enters the right atrium of the heart through the vena cava.

- The right atrium pumps the blood down to the right ventricle through the tricuspid valve (this valve has three flaps of tissue).
- The right ventricle pumps the blood out through the pulmonary artery to the lungs.

Oxygenated blood (coming from the lungs) enters the left atrium through the pulmonary veins.

- The left atrium pumps the blood through the bicuspid (two flaps) valve to the left ventricle.
- The left ventricle pumps the blood out to the rest of the body through the aorta.

> **Top Tip!**
> LORD = left oxygenated, right deoxygenated

Valves and muscular walls

- The tricuspid and bicuspid valves ensure that blood does not pass from the ventricles back into the atria.
- The semilunar valves ensure that blood cannot be sucked back into the heart from the pulmonary artery and the aorta.
- The walls of the atria are thin because they pump blood only a short distance.
- The walls of the ventricles are thick because they pump blood a long distance.
- The wall of the left ventricle is very thick because it has to exert a strong pressure to pump blood all the way around the body.

 ## Experiment

To dissect, display and identify a sheep (or ox) heart

1 Identify the front of the heart (it is more rounded than the back).

2 Identify the right- and left-hand sides of the heart (the left-hand side feels firmer).

3 Identify the membrane around the heart (the pericardium).

4 Identify the coronary arteries and veins on the outside of the heart. Also identify the major blood vessels (if they are still in place).

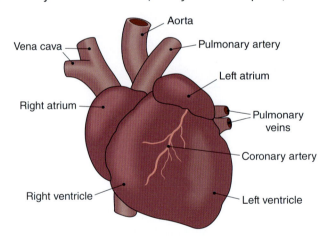

5 Place the heart on a dissecting board.

6 Using a scalpel make four cuts as shown in the diagram (1–4).

7 Using a scissors cut the atria, the pulmonary artery and the aorta as shown (5–8).

8 Note the thin walls of the atria.

9 Note how the walls of the ventricles are thicker.

10 Note that the left ventricle has the thickest wall.

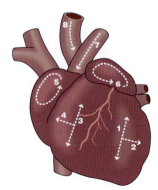

11 Observe the flaps of the valves (they appear white and almost transparent).

12 Note the tendons attached to the valves (they look like white strings).

13 Note the semilunar valves at the point where the aorta and pulmonary artery emerge from the heart.

14 Observe the origin of the coronary artery in the aorta just above the semilunar valve.

15 Identify and flag label all of the parts.

Double circulation

The heart is a double pump. The left-hand side pumps blood to the lungs (the pulmonary circuit), while the right-hand side pumps blood around the rest of the body (the systemic circuit).

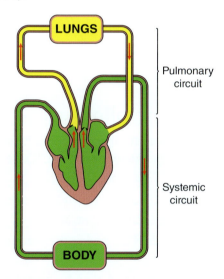

The advantages of double circulation are:

- Oxygen-rich and oxygen-poor blood are separated
- Blood pressure is high enough to reach all parts of the body.

The stages of a heartbeat

Diastole **refers to when heart muscle is relaxed.** *Systole* **is when the heart is contracted.**

There are three stages in the cardiac cycle, i.e. in the events of a single heartbeat.

1 Blood enters the heart

- Due to the pressure exerted by the previous heartbeat, blood enters the atria.
- At this stage the atria and ventricles are relaxed (in diastole).
- All the valves are closed.

2   Blood is pumped to the ventricles

   • The atria contract (atrial systole).
   • The tricuspid and bicuspid valves are forced open.
   • Blood is pumped from the atria to the ventricles.

3   Blood is pumped from the heart

   • The ventricles contract (ventricular systole).
   • The tricuspid and bicuspid valves are forced shut.
   • The semilunar valves are forced open.
   • Blood is pumped out of the heart to the lungs and body.

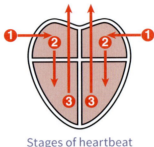

Stages of heartbeat

How heartbeat is controlled

The **pacemaker** (also called the sino-atrial or S-A node) is located in the right atrium. Its function is to control the rate of heartbeat. It does this in the following manner.

   • The pacemaker sends out electrical pulses about every 0.8 seconds.
   • The electrical pulses cause the atria to contract.
   • The atrio-ventricular (A-V) node is located at the junction of the atria and ventricles.
   • When an electrical pulse reaches the A-V node the pulse is strengthened and sent down special tissue located in the septum.
   • The electrical impulses pass out along specialised fibres and cause the walls of the ventricles to contract.

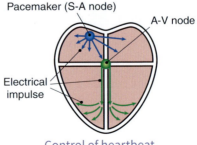

Control of heartbeat

Changing rate of heartbeat

Nerves link the pacemaker to the brain. This allows the rate of heartbeat to be altered.

- The rate of heartbeat is increased by factors such as exercise, excitement and drugs (such as caffeine).
- The rate of heartbeat is decreased by factors such as rest, sleep and drugs (such as alcohol).

Human circulatory system

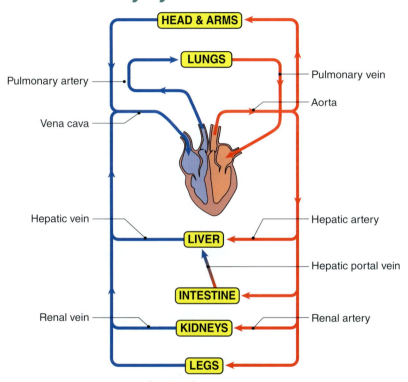

The circulatory system

Portal system

A *portal system* is one in which the blood starts and ends in capillaries.

The hepatic portal vein is an example of a portal system.

Pulse

The pulse that we feel in our wrist or neck is caused by the surge of blood in the arteries triggered by ventricular systole. The pulse rate indicates the rate of heartbeat. The normal pulse or heartbeat rate for an adult is 72 per minute.

To investigate the effect of exercise on the pulse rate

1. Locate a pulse in the wrist or neck.
2. Count the number of pulses per minute while at rest. *(The pulse rate is a measure of the heart rate; the resting pulse rate is used as a control.)*
3. Repeat step 2 twice more and calculate the average pulse rate per minute at rest. *(This acts as a control.)*
4. Exercise gently for 2 minutes.
5. Count the number of pulses per minute until the rate returns to the resting pulse rate.
6. Exercise vigorously for 2 minutes.
7. Count the number of pulses per minute until the rate returns to the resting pulse rate.
8. Compare the resting pulse rate with the rate(s) after exercise.

Top Tip!

There is a choice between this activity and investigating the effect of exercise on the rate of breathing (see page 168).

Blood pressure

Blood pressure is recorded by measuring the pressure needed to stop the flow of blood in the arteries of the upper arm.

- Normal blood pressure is in the order of $^{120}\!/_{80}$ mm of mercury.
- The upper value is systolic pressure while the lower value is diastolic pressure.
- High blood pressure occurs when the lower value is over 95 mm of mercury.
- High blood pressure indicates that the heart has to pump harder to get sufficient blood around the body. In time this may lead to heart attacks.

Lifestyle and the heart

Smoking cigarettes is bad for the heart and circulatory system because:

- Nicotine increases the heart rate and raises blood pressure
- Carbon monoxide reduces the ability of the blood to carry oxygen
- Chemicals in smoke increase the risk of blood clots.

Diet may affect the heart in three ways:

- A fat-rich diet increases the chance of the arteries becoming blocked (which in turn leads to heart attacks)
- Too much salt raises the blood pressure
- Being severely overweight increases blood pressure and results in heart attacks.

Exercise:

- Enlarges and strengthens the heart
- Causes loss of weight.

The Lymphatic System

Learning objectives

In this chapter you will learn about:

1 The lymphatic system
2 The formation of lymph
3 The functions of the lymphatic system

The lymphatic system

The lymphatic system is a second circulatory system. It consists of a colourless fluid called lymph that is forced through a system of tubes called lymph vessels.

Lymph moves very slowly in lymph vessels and is pumped by the action of ordinary body muscles.

The formation of lymph

- The blood in arteries is under high pressure. This causes some fluid to be forced out of plasma in capillaries that connect to arterioles.

- The fluid forced out of the plasma surrounds every cell in the body and is called **tissue fluid**. This fluid is essential because it allows molecules to pass in and out of cells.

- Most of the tissue fluid re-enters the blood in capillaries located nearer to the veins. The blood pressure is slightly lower in these capillaries.

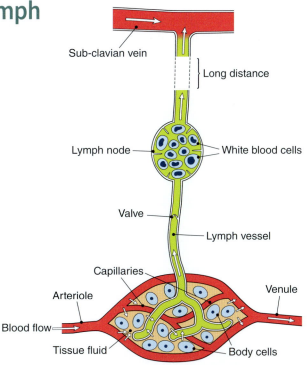

The formation of lymph

- Some of the tissue fluid passes into lymph vessels. The fluid is then called lymph.
- Lymph is moved through lymph vessels by the contraction of body muscles. Valves prevent lymph from flowing in the wrong direction.
- Lymph flows (slowly) through a series of lymph vessels and eventually rejoins the bloodstream near the neck.

Lymph nodes

- Lymph vessels have small swellings called **lymph nodes** along their length. Clusters of lymph nodes (often called glands) are found near the nose (adenoids), throat (tonsils), armpits, chest, appendix and groin.
- Lymph nodes contain large numbers of white blood cells (lymphocytes). They filter and destroy pathogens by engulfing them or by producing antibodies.

The functions of the lymphatic system

- To collect tissue fluid and return it to the bloodstream (if it fails to do this properly, swelling occurs)
- To fight infection by:
    - Filtering pathogens in lymph nodes
    - Maturing and storing lymphocytes
    - Destroying pathogens by engulfing them or by forming antibodies
- To absorb and transport fatty acids and glycerol (each villus contains a lacteal that is full of lymph).

Animal Nutrition

Learning objectives

In this chapter you will learn about:

1 Types of nutrition
2 Events in human nutrition
3 The digestive system (or alimentary canal)
4 A balanced diet

Types of nutrition

Nutrition **is the way in which an organism gets and uses its food.**

There are two types of nutrition: autotrophic and heterotrophic.

1 *Autotrophic* **means that an organism makes its own food.**
   Plants, seaweeds and some bacteria are autotrophs.

2 *Heterotrophic* **means that an organism takes in food from its environment.**
   Animals, fungi, amoeba and some bacteria are heterotrophs.

There are three types of heterotroph.

1 *Herbivores* **are animals that feed only on plants.**
   Cattle, sheep and rabbits are herbivores.

2 *Carnivores* **(or flesh eaters) are animals that feed on other animals.**
   Dogs and cats are carnivores.

3 *Omnivores* **are animals that feed on plants and animals.**
   Badgers and humans are omnivores.

Events in human nutrition

Ingestion **is the taking of food into the mouth.**

Digestion **is the physical and chemical breakdown of food.**
Digestion is necessary to allow small molecules of food to be absorbed through the walls of the intestines.

- Food is physically digested by the teeth, by churning in the stomach and by the action of bile.

- Food is chemically digested by enzymes.

Absorption occurs when food passes from the small intestine into the blood or lymphatic system.

Egestion is the removal of unabsorbed waste from the digestive system.

The digestive system (or alimentary canal)

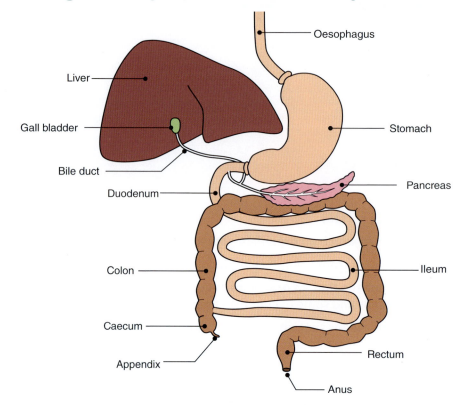

The mouth

Physical digestion is the breakdown of food by mechanical methods.

Physical digestion is carried out by the teeth. There are four types of teeth:

- Incisors are at the front of the mouth and have sharp chiselled edges. They are used to cut and slice food.
- Canines are long, pointed and fang-like. They grip and tear food.
- Premolars and molars are larger teeth that are used to chew and crush food.

The human dental formula tells us the number of each type of tooth in one side of the mouth. The dental formula for an adult is

$$2(I\tfrac{2}{2} \ \ C\tfrac{1}{1} \ \ P\tfrac{2}{2} \ \ M\tfrac{3}{3}) \quad \text{(total = 32)}$$

where I = incisor, C = canine, P = premolar, M = molar.

Chemical digestion **is the breakdown of food using enzymes.** Chemical digestion is carried out in the mouth by the enzyme amylase. This is contained in saliva, which is produced in the salivary glands. The pH of the mouth is between 7 and 8. This pH allows amylase to work. Amylase digests starch to maltose.

$$\text{Starch} \xrightarrow{\text{Amylase}} \text{Maltose}$$

The oesophagus

The oesophagus, along with the rest of the alimentary canal, is made of involuntary muscle. Regular contractions of this muscle push food along the alimentary canal.

Peristalsis **is a wave of muscular action that pushes food through the alimentary canal.**

Peristalsis forces food through the oesophagus to the stomach. Fibre or roughage is essential in the diet in order to stimulate peristalsis.

The stomach

The stomach is a muscular bag in which food remains for 2–4 hours.

Physical digestion

- Physical digestion occurs when the stomach churns the food.
- This helps to turn the food into a liquid called chyme.
- Physical digestion increases the surface area of the food so that enzymes can digest the food more easily.

Chemical digestion

- Chemical digestion occurs due to the action of a number of enzymes.
- **Pepsinogen** is an inactive enzyme that is formed by glands in the lining of the stomach. It is activated to form pepsin in the stomach by hydrochloric acid. Other glands in the lining of the stomach produce hydrochloric acid, which causes the pH of the stomach to be highly acidic (about pH 2). Acid in the stomach kills many bacteria and digests some foods.
- **Pepsin** digests proteins to peptides. Pepsin is a protease, i.e. a protein-digesting enzyme.

$$\text{Protein} \xrightarrow{\text{Pepsin}} \text{Peptides}$$

The stomach is prevented from being digested by pepsin and acid because:

- It is lined with protective mucus
- Pepsin becomes active only when it mixes with acid in the stomach.

The small intestine

The small intestine is small in diameter (about 3 cm) but is a very long tube (about 6 m). It has two main parts: the duodenum and the ileum.

Duodenum

The duodenum is the first 25 cm of the small intestine.

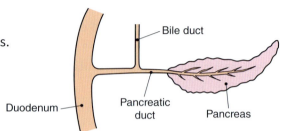

- Food is forced forwards and backwards through the duodenum due to peristalsis.
- The lining of the duodenum produces a large range of enzymes.
- The function of the duodenum is **digestion**.
- The products of the liver and pancreas enter the duodenum.

The pancreas

- The pancreas produces the hormone insulin and enzymes such as amylase and lipase. These enzymes flow down the pancreatic duct and act in the duodenum.
- Pancreatic amylase has the same function as salivary amylase. It is produced to replace salivary amylase that was destroyed (denatured) by the acid in the stomach.

$$\textbf{Starch} \xrightarrow{\textbf{Amylase}} \textbf{Maltose}$$

- Lipase digests fats to form fatty acids and glycerol.

$$\textbf{Fats} \xrightarrow{\textbf{Lipase}} \textbf{Fatty acids + glycerol}$$

The liver

- The liver is the only organ that gets its blood from two major vessels: the hepatic artery and the hepatic portal vein.
- Blood leaves the liver in the hepatic vein.

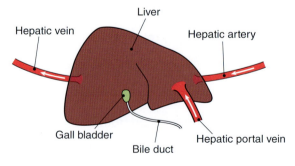

The liver and its blood vessels

Functions

- Breaking down old red blood cells
- Forming bile
- Breaking down (detoxifying) poisons
- Breaking down unwanted amino acids to form urea (deamination)
- Converting glucose to glycogen

- Converting excess carbohydrate to fat
- Storing vitamins and minerals
- Forming plasma proteins such as clotting proteins
- Forming cholesterol (used to make hormones)
- Producing heat to warm the blood.

Bile

Bile is a yellow-green liquid formed from the breakdown of red blood cells.

Bile is:

- Made in the liver
- Composed of water, bile salts and bile pigments
- Stored in the gall bladder
- Released into the duodenum through the bile duct.

The functions of bile are:

- To emulsify fats, i.e. to break large blobs of fat into smaller particles
- To neutralise the acid coming from the stomach
- To eliminate bile pigments from the body.

Summary of enzymes

Enzyme	Made in	pH	Substrate	Product
Amylase	Salivary glands or pancreas	7–8	Starch	Maltose
Pepsin	Stomach	2	Protein	Peptides
Lipase	Pancreas	7–8	Fat	Fatty acids and glycerol

Final products of digestion

Food leaving the duodenum has been fully digested as follows:

Food	Digested to
Carbohydrates	Glucose
Proteins	Amino acids
Fats	Fatty acids and glycerol

Ileum

The ileum is the second part of the small intestine.

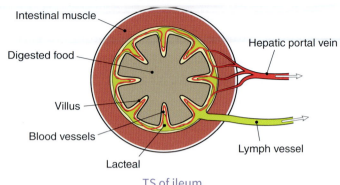

- The function of the ileum is **absorption**.
- The ileum has numerous infoldings called villi (singular: villus). These increase the surface area for absorption.
- The villi have numerous micro-villi.
- The lining of the villi is only one cell thick.

Absorption in the ileum

- **Glucose and amino acids** pass through the villi walls and into the bloodstream by diffusion. They are then carried to the liver by the hepatic portal vein.
- **Fatty acids and glycerol** are enclosed in a covering and pass into lacteals. Each lacteal is located in the centre of a villus. The lacteals contain a liquid called lymph.
- The fatty acids and glycerol are carried by lymph vessels and pass into the bloodstream near the neck. The coating is removed and the fats pass into body cells.

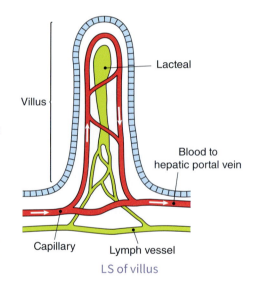

Adaptations of the small intestine

- It is made of muscle (allows peristalsis, moves food along).
- The duodenum produces many enzymes (improve digestion).
- It is very long (to increase surface area for improved absorption).
- It contains villi and micro-villi (to increase surface area for improved absorption).
- The villi have thin walls (to improve absorption).
- The villi are covered by many blood vessels (to transport the absorbed food).
- Each villus contains a lacteal (to allow lipids to be absorbed).

The large intestine

The large intestine is large in diameter (about 6 cm) but is only 1.5 m long.

- The function of the large intestine is to **reabsorb water**. This happens mainly in the colon.
- The functions of the caecum and appendix are not fully understood.
- Semi-solid waste (called faeces) is stored in the rectum and egested through the anus.

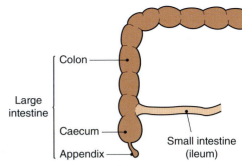

The structure of the large intestine

Symbiotic bacteria in the intestines

The large intestine contains a huge number of bacterial cells. (There are more bacteria in the intestines than human cells in the entire body!)

These bacteria are of benefit in the following ways:

- Some of them produce B group vitamins and vitamin K
- Other bacteria break down small amounts of cellulose.

Both of these types of bacteria are symbiotic or mutualistic (i.e. they live in close association with us, and both humans and bacteria benefit).

A balanced diet

A balanced diet contains all the necessary nutrients in the correct proportions.

The nutrients include:

- Carbohydrates, proteins, fats
- Vitamins, minerals
- Fibre and water.

The total amount of food eaten depends on a number of factors such as:

- Age (young people need more food than older people)
- Activity levels (active people need more food than inactive people)
- Gender (males need more food than females)
- Health (those who are ill use and need less energy than those who are healthy).

Food groups

Food can be arranged into four food groups. The number of times that each food group should be eaten each day is given in brackets.

- Cereals, bread and potatoes (6)
- Fruit and vegetables (4)
- Milk, cheese and yoghurt (4)
- Meat, fish and beans (2).

Foods and drinks such as lipids, cakes, biscuits, sweets, sugars, soft drinks, salt and alcohol should not be consumed too regularly.

29 Homeostasis and Excretion

Learning objectives

In this chapter you will learn about:

1 Homeostasis

2 Temperature regulation in humans

3 The skin

4 Excretion

5 The urinary system

6 Nephrons

7 Control of urine volume

Homeostasis

Homeostasis **is the ability of an organism to maintain a constant internal environment.**

Homeostasis is necessary to allow organisms to survive efficiently in environments that are changing all the time. Organisms need to control their internal environment to allow metabolism. The internal environment for humans consists mainly of tissue fluid that surrounds all the cells in the body. By controlling this fluid the contents of the body cells can be controlled.

Examples of homeostasis in humans and the organs and systems involved

Example	Organ or system
Maintaining a body temperature of 37°C	Body temperature is mainly controlled by the skin.
Maintaining the pH of the blood and tissue fluid close to 7	Blood and tissue fluid pH is controlled by the kidneys.
Preventing the accumulation of waste in the body	Elimination of waste is controlled by the kidneys, skin and lungs.
Maintaining the correct concentration of oxygen	Oxygen (and carbon dioxide) concentrations are controlled by the breathing system.
Maintaining the correct glucose concentration	Glucose concentration is controlled by the endocrine system.

Homeostasis allows conditions in the body to be changed **slightly** at different times, as outlined below.

- Body temperature falls by about 1°C when we sleep.
- Body temperature rises when we have an infection.
- Blood glucose concentration rises rapidly when we get a fright (caused by the hormone adrenalin).
- Hormonal changes during the menstrual cycle and puberty alter the internal environment of the body.

Temperature regulation in humans

Temperature affects the rate of enzyme action. To control the rate of enzyme reactions it is important to control body temperature. Animals do this in two ways.

Ectotherms **are animals that gain or lose heat from their environment.** Ectotherms were formerly called cold-blooded. They include animals such as frogs, snakes and lizards. The temperature of an ectotherm changes with the external temperature.

Endotherms **are animals that generate their own heat by metabolic reactions.**

Endotherms were formerly called warm-blooded. They include humans, dogs and birds, who all maintain constant body temperatures.

The skin

The skin plays a major role in controlling the temperature of the body.

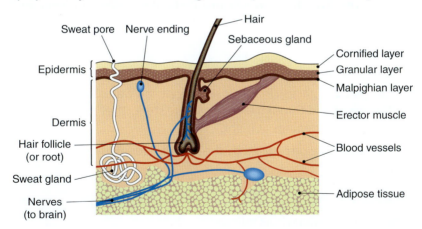

Parts of the skin

The outer **epidermis** consists of the following layers:

- The outer cornified layer contains cells full of keratin. Most of these cells are dead.
- The inner epidermis contains a granular layer, where keratin is formed.

- The Malpighian layer contains cells that are constantly dividing by mitosis to replace cells lost from the cornified layer. The Malpighian layer also produces melanin (the brown pigment that causes suntan). Melanin absorbs ultraviolet rays, which may cause cancer.

The **dermis** contains sweat glands, nerve endings, sebaceous glands and blood vessels.

The innermost layer of **adipose tissue** is full of fat-rich cells.

Temperature regulation by the skin

In **cold conditions** the skin retains heat as follows:

- Erector muscles contract (forming goose pimples). This causes the hairs to stand up and trap a layer of warm air close to the skin. The way in which hairs stand up is called **piloerection**.
- Blood vessels in the skin contract, causing the skin to turn white. This means that less heat is lost to the outside. This is called **vasoconstriction**.

In **warm conditions** the skin reduces temperature as follows:

- Sweat is produced. When sweat (or perspiration) evaporates it removes heat from the body. It is necessary to replace this loss of salt and water by drinking fluids, especially when we perspire heavily.
- Blood vessels in the skin enlarge (**vasodilation**). This results in more blood flowing close to the surface (blushing) with a resulting loss of heat.

Excretion

Excretion **is the removal of the waste products of metabolism from an organism.**

Excretion in plants

'Excretion' is a term normally associated with animals. The equivalent term in plants is 'loss of waste' (gases). Plants lose oxygen and water vapour through stomata in the leaves and through lenticels in the stem. They may also lose carbon dioxide through these openings at night.

However, these gases are often used by the plant for respiration (O_2) and photosynthesis (CO_2).

Excretion and homeostasis

Excretion helps in homeostasis as follows:

- It removes excess water, salts and wastes from the body
- By controlling the salt/water balance it acts to regulate osmosis.

Organs of excretion in humans

- The skin (excretes salts and water as sweat)
- The lungs (excrete carbon dioxide and water)
- The kidneys (excrete water, salts and urea in the form of urine).

The urinary system

Urea

- Proteins are digested to amino acids. We use some of these amino acids but many of them are surplus to our needs.

- Excess amino acids may become poisonous. To prevent this from happening they are taken to our **liver** where they are broken down (deaminated) to form urea.

Urea is a nitrogen-containing salt. It is carried out of the liver in our bloodstream.

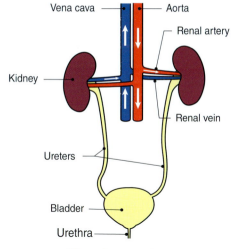

The urinary system

Parts of the urinary system

- The **renal arteries** carry blood that is high in waste products (salts, urea and water) from the aorta to each kidney.

- The **kidneys** carry out three functions.

  — They **filter** waste products from the blood (this happens in the cortex).

  — They **reabsorb** useful materials from the filtrate (this happens in the cortex and medulla).

  — They **secrete** some substances from the blood into the filtrate (this happens in the cortex).

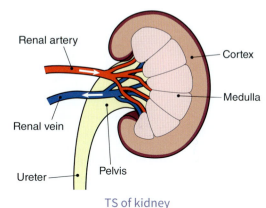

TS of kidney

- The **renal veins** carry purified blood from the kidneys back to the vena cava for circulation around the body.

- Urine is formed in the kidneys.

- The two ureters carry urine to the bladder.

- The **bladder** stores urine.

- The **urethra** carries urine out of the body.

Nephrons

Nephrons are the structures in the kidney that make urine. Each kidney has over one million nephrons.

A nephron is a coiled tube, about 3 cm long, which is open at one end. The nephrons are located mainly in the cortex of the kidney. However, the **loop of Henle** projects down into the medulla while the collecting ducts enter the pelvis.

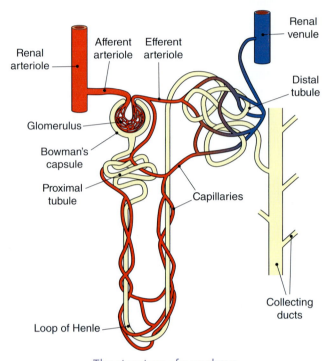

The structure of a nephron

The formation of the urine in the nephron

- Blood in the renal artery is high in wastes.
- The renal artery forms many smaller renal **arterioles**.
- Each renal arteriole forms a number of **afferent arterioles**. Each of these arterioles enters a cup-shaped structure called **Bowman's capsule**.
- Each afferent arteriole subdivides to form a network of small capillaries called a **glomerulus**.
- The blood pressure in the glomerulus is much higher than normal for the following reasons:
  - The blood in an arteriole is under high pressure
  - The incoming afferent arteriole is wide
  - The outgoing efferent arteriole is narrower (the difference in size increases the already high pressure).

- The high pressure causes **filtration**. This form of filtration is often called ultra-filtration or high-pressure filtration.
- Small molecules such as water, glucose, amino acids, vitamins, minerals, salts and urea are forced into Bowman's capsule (they form a liquid called glomerular filtrate).
- Large substances such as proteins and blood cells do not enter Bowman's capsule.

- In the **proximal (convoluted) tubule**:
  - water is reabsorbed by osmosis
  - glucose, amino acids, vitamins and minerals are reabsorbed by a combination of diffusion and active transport.

Active transport **is the movement of molecules using energy against a concentration gradient (i.e. it can move molecules from a low concentration to a high concentration).**

- In the descending limb of the **loop of Henle**, water is reabsorbed by osmosis.
- In the ascending limb of the **loop of Henle**, salts are reabsorbed into the medulla of the kidney by a combination of diffusion and active transport.
- In the **distal (convoluted) tubule**:
  - Water is reabsorbed by osmosis
  - Some salts are reabsorbed by diffusion and active transport
  - Secretion of salts and hydrogen ions (H^+) from the blood into the tubule helps to control the pH of the blood.
- In the **collecting duct**, water is reabsorbed by osmosis (due to the high salt concentration in the cells of the medulla).
  The liquid leaving the collecting ducts is called urine.

Control of urine volume

A hormone called **anti-diuretic hormone (ADH)** controls the volume of water reabsorbed in the collecting ducts (and in the distal tubules to a smaller extent). ADH is produced in the hypothalamus and then passes into the pituitary gland.

Low water content in plasma

- If we do not drink enough water or if we consume too much salt (i.e. if we are thirsty) the water level in the blood plasma is **too low**.
- In this case we release ADH. This causes the collecting ducts to become more permeable to water.
- Extra water is reabsorbed into the blood. The plasma gains water and becomes less salty.
- The volume of urine produced is lowered.

Normal water content in plasma

- When the water content of the plasma returns to normal, ADH is no longer released.
- The collecting ducts stop reabsorbing water so that the plasma does not become more diluted.
- The volume of urine produced increases.

Summary

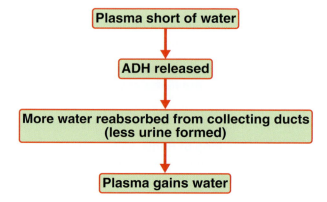

Human Breathing

30

Learning objectives

In this chapter you will learn about:

1 **The respiratory system**
2 **The mechanism of breathing**
3 **A breathing disorder**

The respiratory system

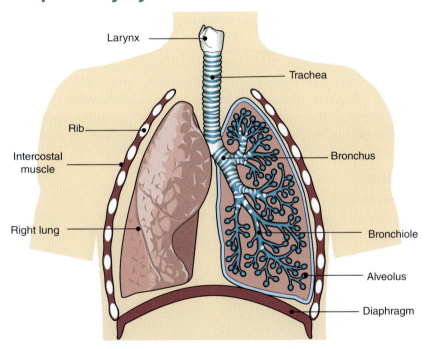

Nose

We breathe in through the nose because it cleans, moistens and warms the air. Air that is warm and moist can diffuse more easily from the lungs into the bloodstream.

Pharynx

The **epiglottis** is located in the pharynx (or throat) at the top of the trachea. The epiglottis closes over the trachea when we swallow to prevent food and drink from passing into the lungs.

Larynx

The larynx (or voice box) is located in the trachea just below the epiglottis.

Trachea

- The trachea (or windpipe), along with its subdivisions the bronchi and the upper bronchioles, is made of muscle and elastic fibres as well as c-shaped sections of inflexible cartilage.
- The lower bronchioles do not have cartilage. This allows them to contract and narrow, leading to conditions such as asthma.
- All of these tubes are lined with mucus and cilia. Disease-causing organisms (pathogens) stick to the mucus. The cilia beat to create a current that pushes mucus up to the epiglottis. Mucus then passes down to the stomach.

Lungs

The function of the lungs is gas exchange. The lungs are enclosed by two pleural membranes. A layer of liquid located between the pleural membranes helps to protect the lungs from being damaged by rubbing against the chest cavity (or thorax).

Alveolus (plural: alveoli)

The trachea divides to form two bronchi. Each bronchus enters a lung. Each bronchus divides to form about one million bronchioles. Each bronchiole ends in a dead-end sac called an alveolus. There are about 350 million alveoli in each lung. The function of the alveoli is gas exchange. They are adapted for this function because they:

- Are very numerous
- Have a large surface area
- Have thin walls
- Have moist surfaces to increase diffusion
- Have a rich blood supply to carry gases away from the lungs.

Gas exchange

In each alveolus:

- Oxygen passes from the alveolus into red blood cells (where it is transported as oxyhaemoglobin)
- Carbon dioxide passes from the plasma into the alveolus

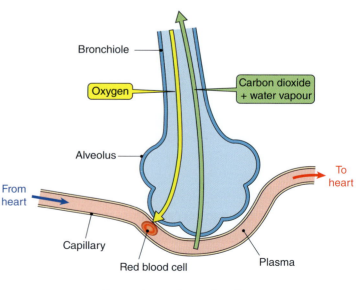

Gas exchange in an alveolus

- Water vapour passes from the plasma into the alveolus.

Gas exchange in the lungs results in the following changes between inhaled and exhaled air.

	Inhaled	Exhaled
Oxygen %	21	14
Carbon dioxide %	0.04	5.6
Water vapour	Lower	Higher

The mechanism of breathing

Inhalation

Top Tip!

Carbon dioxide levels in the blood control the rate of breathing.

1 Respiration in all our body cells produces the waste gas carbon dioxide. This is a slightly acidic gas.

2 Respiratory centres in the medulla oblongata in the brain monitor the acidity of the blood. When the acidity level is too high (due to CO_2), electrical impulses are sent from the medulla to the diaphragm and intercostal muscles.

3 The diaphragm and intercostal muscles contract. For this reason inhalation is said to be an **active** process (i.e. energy is required).

4 The ribs move up and out, the diaphragm moves down.

5 The volume of the chest increases.

6 The pressure in the chest falls.

7 The external air pressure is now greater than the air pressure in the chest.

8 Air is forced into the lungs, causing them to inflate.

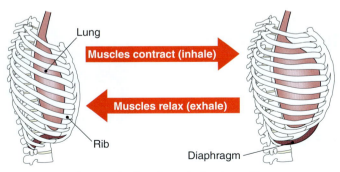

Lung

Muscles contract (inhale)

Muscles relax (exhale)

Rib

Diaphragm

Changes in the chest during breathing

Exhalation

1 Breathing out involves the reverse of points 3 to 8 above.

2 Exhalation is a **passive** process because the muscles only have to relax (this does not involve the use of energy).

Effects of exercise on the rate of breathing

- Exercise requires energy. Therefore exercise increases the rate of respiration. This in turn means that more CO_2 is produced.

- The increased level of CO_2 increases the rate of breathing. This means that more CO_2 is breathed out to reduce the level of CO_2 in the body.

- The increased rate of breathing also means that more oxygen passes into the body.

 Experiment

To investigate the effect of exercise on the rate of breathing

1 Count the number of inhalations a person takes per minute while at rest *(each inhalation represents one breath)*.

2 Repeat step 1 twice more.

3 Add the three values and divide by 3 to obtain the average breathing rate at rest *(this will be used as the control)*.

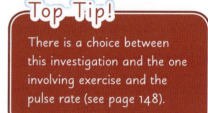

Top Tip!

There is a choice between this investigation and the one involving exercise and the pulse rate (see page 148).

4 Exercise gently (e.g. walk or jog slowly) for 2 minutes.

5 Count the number of inhalations per minute until the breathing rate returns to the resting rate.

6 Exercise vigorously (e.g. run) for 2 minutes.

7 Count the number of inhalations per minute until the rate returns to the resting rate.

8 Compare the rate of breathing at rest with the rates after exercise.

A breathing disorder

Asthma is a breathing disorder affecting about 5% of adults and over 10% of children.

Point to note

Asthma and bronchitis are breathing disorders. You need to study only **one** of these disorders.

Symptoms

The symptoms of asthma are noisy, wheezy breathing along with a feeling of a lack of breath.

Cause

The precise cause of asthma is unknown. However, it can be triggered by inhaling substances (called allergens) such as pollen and dust from animals like cats, dogs and house mites.

The bronchioles become narrow and their linings become inflamed. This reduces the amount of air that can pass in and out of the lungs.

Prevention

If the allergen can be identified and then avoided, it will reduce the severity of the asthma attacks. This may involve avoiding certain foods or pets, putting special covers on mattresses, staying indoors during times of high pollen counts and using inhalers (see below).

Treatment

The normal treatment for asthma is to take drugs (bronchodilators) that widen the bronchioles and reduce inflammation (steroids). These drugs are often taken using inhalers.

31 The Nervous System

Learning objectives

In this chapter you will learn about:

1 Parts of the nervous system

2 Neurons

3 Features of nerve impulses

4 Synapse

5 The central nervous system

6 Reflex action

7 A nervous system disorder

Parts of the nervous system

The nervous system is divided into two parts.

- The central nervous system (CNS) consists of the brain and spinal cord.
- The peripheral nervous system (PNS) consists of nerves that carry impulses to and from the CNS.

Neurons

A *neuron* (or neurone) is a nerve cell. There are three types of neuron.

- A **sensory neuron** carries impulses from receptors in sense organs **to** the CNS.
- A **motor neuron** carries impulses **away from** the CNS to muscles and glands.
- An **interneuron** carries impulses **within** the CNS (i.e. from sensory to motor neurons).

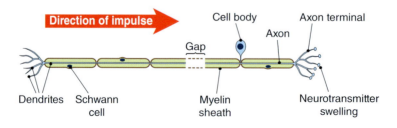

Structure of sensory neuron

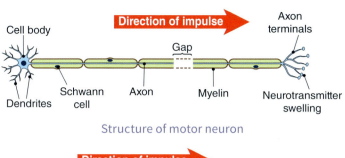

Structure of motor neuron

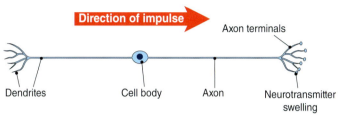

Structure of interneuron

Functions of the parts of the neurons

Part	Function
Dendrites	Receive information and carry electrical impulses **towards** the cell body
Axons	Carry impulses **away from** the cell body
Cell body	Contains a nucleus and forms dendrites and axons
Myelin (sheath)	A fat-rich material that insulates the electrical impulses
Schwann cells	Form the myelin (sheath)
Neurotransmitter swellings	Produce neurotransmitter chemicals

Features of nerve impulses

Movement of the impulse

An impulse travels along a neuron in the form of an electrical impulse.

In order for the electrical impulse to travel it is necessary for ions (charged particles such as sodium, potassium and chloride) to move in and out of the dendrites and axons. The movement of these ions requires energy in the form of ATP.

Threshold

The *threshold* is the least possible stimulus needed to send an impulse. An impulse will pass along a neuron if it receives a stimulus of sufficient strength. If the stimulus is below the threshold it will fail to cause an impulse to pass.

All or nothing rule

The all or nothing rule means that:

- If the threshold is reached, an impulse is sent
- If the threshold is not reached, no impulse is sent.

This means that there are only two possibilities: an impulse travels or it does not.

Same speed

All impulses travel at the same speed. There is no such thing as a fast or a slow impulse.

However, impulses travel faster when the neuron is insulated with myelin than when it is not insulated.

Delay (or refractory period)

There is a tiny delay between one impulse and a following impulse. This delay is to allow the message to pass from one neuron to another at the synapse.

Unidirectional

Impulses can travel only from sensory to motor neurons. This is because of the events (explained below) that occur at the synapse.

Synapse

A *synapse* is the region where two neurons come into close contact. A *synaptic cleft* is a tiny gap between two neurons.

Events at a synapse

There is an electrical → chemical → electrical inter-conversion at each synapse.

- When an electrical impulse arrives at a synapse it stimulates the release of neurotransmitter chemicals. These chemicals are made and stored in the neurotransmitter swellings (or vesicles). These swellings are found on only one side of the synapse (i.e. they are on the sensory neuron).
- A wide range of neurotransmitter chemicals is made by the nervous system. Examples include acetylcholine and dopamine.
- The chemicals diffuse across the synaptic cleft.
- When the chemicals enter the motor neuron they are broken down and an electrical impulse is regenerated.

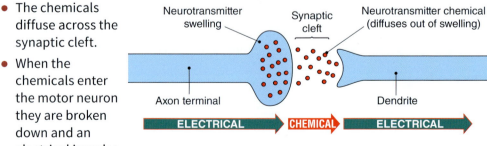

A synapse

Function of synapse

The main function of a synapse is to **control the direction** of impulses in the nervous system (i.e. they act as valves). For example, impulses flow only from sensory to motor neurons.

The central nervous system

The central nervous system (CNS) consists of the brain and spinal cord.

Both of these are protected by the bones of the skull and backbone and are enclosed by three membranes called the meninges. A protective fluid called cerebrospinal fluid is located between the inner two meninges.

The CNS contains huge numbers of neurons.

- The cell bodies are grey in colour.
- The myelin sheath surrounding dendrites and axons gives them a white colour.

The brain

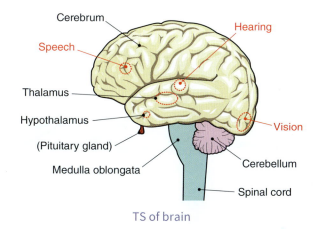

TS of brain

Cerebrum

The cerebrum is the largest and most advanced part of the brain. It controls conscious movement, the senses, intelligence, personality, logic and emotions.

The cerebrum is divided into two halves called cerebral hemispheres. These are connected by a structure called the corpus callosum.

- The left hemisphere controls the right-hand side of the body as well as language, mathematics and logic.
- The right hemisphere controls the left-hand side of the body as well as art, music, shapes and emotions.

Cerebellum

The cerebellum controls balance and muscular coordination.

Medulla

The medulla oblongata controls involuntary muscles such as the intercostal muscles, the diaphragm and intestinal muscles.

Thalamus and hypothalamus

The thalamus is a sorting centre for the brain. Incoming impulses are directed to the correct part of the brain by the thalamus.

The hypothalamus controls the internal environment of the body (homeostasis). This means that it regulates features such as hunger, thirst, temperature and blood pressure. (The **pituitary gland** is not a part of the brain. It is linked to and controlled by the hypothalamus. It produces hormones and is dealt with in Chapter 33.)

The spinal cord

The backbone encloses the spinal cord. The spinal cord carries impulses to and from the brain. It is also involved in reflex actions (see opposite).

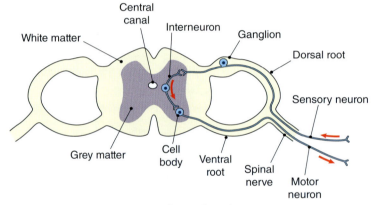

TS of spinal cord

Part of the spinal cord	Functions
Meninges	Surround and control entry of materials to the (brain and) spinal cord
Spinal nerves	Thirty-one pairs of spinal nerves carry impulses to and from the spinal cord
Dorsal root	Carries impulses into the spinal cord along sensory neurons
Ganglion	A ganglion (plural: ganglia) is a swelling that contains the cell bodies of sensory neurons
White matter	Contains axons
Grey matter	Contains cell bodies
Central canal	Contains a fluid called cerebrospinal fluid
Ventral root	Carries impulses out of the spinal cord along motor neurons

Reflex action

A *reflex action* is an automatic, unconscious or involuntary response to a stimulus. The brain is not involved in reflex actions.

Examples

Examples of reflex actions are the knee jerk, blinking for protection, raising your hands when falling and dropping a hot object.

Significance

The benefit of reflex actions is that they allow faster responses than normal.

For this reason they **protect** the body from harm.

The path of a reflex action

The path taken by the electrical impulses in a reflex action is called a reflex arc. The following description relates to dropping a hot object.

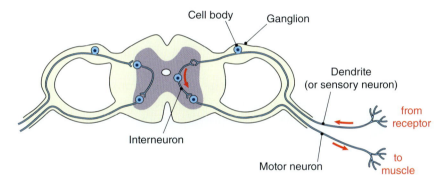

1   Receptors in the finger detect the hot object.

2   An impulse travels along a sensory neuron to the spinal cord.

3   The impulse travels into the spine through the dorsal root.

4   In the spinal cord the impulse splits.

   (a) It crosses a synapse onto an interneuron.

   (b) It crosses another synapse and passes on up to the brain.

5   From the interneuron the impulse crosses another synapse and travels out of the ventral root along a motor neuron.

6   The motor neuron connects to a muscle that causes the response. Note that the brain did not cause this response.

7   As the response is being carried out, the brain becomes aware of why the response was necessary (due to the impulse at 4(b) above).

A nervous system disorder

Parkinson's disease

Cause

The cause of Parkinson's disease is a failure to produce a neurotransmitter called dopamine. This failure occurs in a tiny section of the brain that controls muscle movements.

The reasons for failing to produce dopamine are not known. The disease is most common in older people and in males.

The symptoms of Parkinson's are:

- Trembling of the hands and legs
- Muscular stiffness
- Difficulty in walking.

Prevention

Given that the causes are unknown, there is no way of preventing or curing the disease.

Treatment

Treatment involves physiotherapy and special exercises along with the use of special aids. Drug treatment may be of limited use but works for only a short time. There are great hopes that stem cells may provide a cure.

The Senses

32

Learning objectives

In this chapter you will learn about:

1 The senses
2 The eye
3 The ear
4 A hearing disorder

The senses

There are five senses: touch, taste, smell, sight and hearing.

Some claims are made that balance is also a sense, while the sense of touch involves pressure, pain and temperature.

Sense	Organ	Stimulus
Touch	Skin	Touch and temperature
Taste	Tongue and lining of the throat	Dissolved chemicals (sweet, sour, salty and bitter)
Smell	Nose	Chemicals in the gas state
Sight	Eyes	Light
Hearing	Ears	Sound

The eye

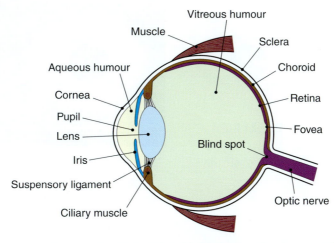

Part	Function
The sclera or sclerotic coat	A tough, white, outer coat that holds the eye in shape
The choroid	A dark-brown or black layer that contains blood vessels that nourish the eye; it also absorbs any light that passes through the retina to prevent light from being reflected within the eye
The retina	A light-sensitive layer that contains receptors called rods and cones
The fovea	Located in the centre of the retina; cones are concentrated here; images are formed here when we look at an object
Optic nerve	Carries impulses from the eye to the brain
Blind spot	There are no rods or cones at the blind spot; we cannot see any image formed here
Cornea	A transparent section of the eye that allows light in
Lens	Changes shape to focus light on the retina
Ciliary muscle	Changes the shape of the lens
Suspensory ligaments	Connect the ciliary muscle to the lens
Iris	The coloured part of the eye; it controls the amount of light entering the eye
Pupil	The black circle in the centre of the eye: it allows light into the eye
The aqueous and vitreous humours	Liquids that support the eye

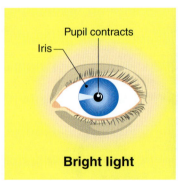

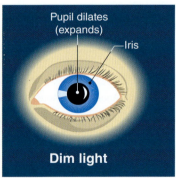

The eye in bright light   The eye in dim light

The following table outlines the differences between rods and cones.

	Rods	Cones
Shape	Rod-shaped	Cone-shaped
Detect	Black and white	Colours (red, green and blue)
Active in	Dim light	Bright light
Location	All over the retina	At the fovea
Number per eye	120 million	6 million

The ear

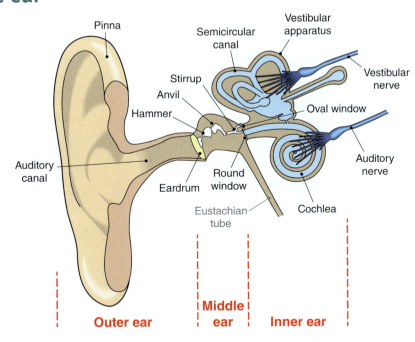

Outer ear

The outer ear is filled with air.

- The **pinna** is made of cartilage. It collects vibrations in the air and channels them into the ear.
- The **auditory canal** carries vibrations to the eardrum.

- The **eardrum** is a tightly stretched membrane that vibrates when stimulated by vibrations in the auditory canal.

Middle ear

The middle ear is filled with air.

- The **ossicles** are three bones called the hammer, anvil and stirrup. The stirrup is the smallest bone in the body. They increase (amplify) the vibrations and pass them on to the oval window.
- The **Eustachian tube** is not really part of the ear. It is a tube that connects the middle ear to the pharynx (or throat). Its function is to equalise pressure on either side of the eardrum.

Inner ear

The inner ear is filled with a fluid called lymph.

Cochlea

The **cochlea** is a spiral tube similar to a snail's shell. Its function is hearing.

- Vibrations pass into the lymph in the cochlea through a membrane called the oval window.
- As the vibrations pass along the cochlea they stimulate pressure receptors that form a layer called the organ of Corti in the cochlea.
- Impulses pass from these receptors to the cerebrum along the auditory nerve.

Vestibular apparatus

The **three semicircular** canals are all at right angles to one another. They form part of a structure called the vestibular apparatus. Their function is balance.

- Receptors in the semicircular canals detect when our head is not upright or when it is rotating.
- The receptors send impulses to the cerebellum of the brain through the vestibular nerve.

Top Tip!

You are required to know about corrective measures for long and short sight **or** for a hearing defect. A hearing disorder is outlined below.

A hearing disorder (glue ear)

Cause

Glue ear is a hearing disorder caused by too much fluid collecting in the middle ear of (usually) young children. The build-up of fluid is often the result of a viral infection.

Symptoms

Glue ear often causes some loss of hearing as it prevents the three bones in the middle ear from moving properly. It also causes pain or discomfort.

Corrective measures

- In mild cases, decongestant drugs are taken, which break up the fluid and allow it to drain (through the Eustachian tubes).
- In severe cases, grommets are placed in the eardrums. These allow air to enter the middle ear and force the fluid down the Eustachian tubes.

33 The Endocrine System

Learning objectives

In this chapter you will learn about:

1 Exocrine and endocrine glands
2 Hormones
3 Nervous and endocrine coordination
4 The principal endocrine glands
5 Hormone deficiency and excess for thyroxine
6 Control of hormone (thyroxine) production
7 Hormone supplements

Exocrine and endocrine glands

	Exocrine glands	Endocrine glands
Definition	Have ducts or tubes	Have no ducts or tubes
Examples	Sweat, tear, salivary glands, the liver	Pituitary, thyroid, parathyroids, adrenals, pancreas, ovaries or testes

Hormones

A *hormone* is a chemical produced by an endocrine gland and transported in the bloodstream to act in another part of the body.

Many hormones are proteins. However, some hormones (such as those in the reproductive system) are steroid (or lipid) based.

Nervous and endocrine coordination

Hormones are involved in coordinating the body. They interact with the nervous system in achieving this function. The manner in which the two systems are integrated is shown in the following table.

Feature	Endocrine system	Nervous system
Speed of action	Slow-acting	Fast-acting
Length of action	Long-lasting	Short-lived
Type of message	Chemical	Electrical
Speed of message	Slow delivery	Fast delivery
Areas affected	Affects many areas	Affects one area

For example, reproductive hormones are released at puberty. They may take years to work but once they become active, the results (such as the growth of body hair) persist for years.

In contrast, if you decide to click your fingers (coordinated by the nervous system) the result happens within a split second. Once the action has been carried out there is no residual effect.

The principal endocrine glands

Endocrine glands are ductless glands that produce hormones and release them into the bloodstream.

Gland	Hormone	Function
Pituitary	Human growth hormone (HGH)	Elongates bones in the skeleton
Thyroid	Thyroxine	Controls metabolism
Parathyroid	Parathormone	Controls release of calcium from bones
Pancreas	Insulin	Causes glucose to be removed from the blood (it is then stored as glycogen)
Adrenal	Adrenalin	Allows us to respond to stress
Ovaries or testes	Dealt with in Chapter 34	

Pituitary gland

This peanut-sized gland in the middle of the head is controlled by the hypothalamus. The pituitary gland produces many hormones:

- Human growth hormone
- Anti-diuretic hormone (ADH, which regulates the volume of urine)
- Thyroid-stimulating hormone (TSH, dealt with later in this chapter)
- FSH and LH (dealt with in Chapter 34 on human reproduction)

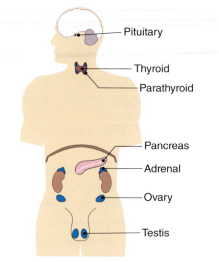

Location of the principal endocrine glands

Parathyroids

The four parathyroids are located in the thyroid gland in the neck. They produce parathormone, which controls the release of calcium from bone. Problems with this hormone can result in brittle bones.

Pancreas

The pancreas is both an exocrine and an endocrine gland.

Endocrine function

The islets of Langerhans are special groups of cells that make insulin. Insulin causes glucose to be absorbed from the bloodstream into cells. In the cells, glucose is then converted to glycogen for storage.

A shortage of insulin results in diabetes (which means that blood sugar levels are too high).

Exocrine function

Most of the cells in the pancreas produce enzymes (such as amylase and lipase). These enzymes pass into the pancreatic duct and become active in the duodenum.

Adrenals

The adrenal glands are located on top of the kidneys in the lower back.

They produce the hormone adrenalin. This is often called the fright/flight/fight hormone. It is produced when we are under stress (fright) and its effects allow us to respond to the stress (fight or flight).

For example, it causes:

- Increased heartbeat and breathing
- The conversion of glycogen to glucose
- Widening of the bronchioles
- Increased blood flow to muscles
- Reduced blood flow to the skin (pale) and intestines ('butterflies')
- Increased mental alertness.

Thyroid

The thyroid makes the hormone thyroxine (or thyroxin). Iodine (which is found in seafood and sea salt) is needed to make thyroxine.

Thyroxine controls metabolism, i.e. the rate of all chemical reactions in the body.

Hormone deficiency and excess for thyroxine

Deficiency of thyroxine

Symptoms

In young children a shortage of thyroxine results in reduced physical and mental development, a condition called cretinism. In adults it results in a reduced metabolic rate, tiredness, reduced mental and physical activity, the build-up of fluid under the skin, and weight gain. In addition, the thyroid gland swells, a condition called goitre.

Treatment

Treatment involves taking tablets of thyroxine or iodine.

Excess of thyroxine

Symptoms

Too much thyroxine causes an increased metabolic rate, which in turn causes hunger, loss of weight, heat production, sweating, bulging eyes and anxiety. This condition may result from an enlarged thyroid (goitre).

Treatment

Treatment may involve removing part of the thyroid or killing part of it using radioactive iodine.

Control of hormone (thyroxine) production

The concentration of thyroxine (and of all other hormones) is controlled by a mechanism called **negative feedback**.

The pituitary gland produces a hormone called TSH (thyroid-stimulating hormone). This is released into the blood and causes the thyroid gland to produce thyroxine (provided it has a supply of iodine). The concentration of thyroxine is controlled as follows:

- If thyroxine levels in the bloodstream are correct, TSH is not produced. As a result no more thyroxine is produced. This means that the correct level of thyroxine has a negative effect. This is called negative feedback.
- If thyroxine levels are below normal, TSH is made. This causes more thyroxine to be produced. When thyroxine levels reach normal again, TSH is inhibited or switched off.

Hormone supplements

Insulin

- The inability to produce insulin (or the inability of cells to absorb insulin) results in diabetes.
- Diabetes results in high glucose concentrations in the blood and urine, production of large volumes of urine, severe thirst, loss of weight and tiredness.
- Diabetes may be controlled by regular (up to four times a day) injections of insulin. Carbohydrate consumption and body weight are also controlled.
- Insulin cannot be taken in tablet form, as it is a protein and would be digested.

Anabolic steroids

- Anabolic steroids mimic the action of the male hormone testosterone. In particular they build up muscle mass in the body, reduce fat, speed up the repair of injuries and form stronger bones.
- They are used (illegally) in sports. The dangers of anabolic steroids are failure of the liver or adrenal glands, the inability to produce offspring (infertility), failure of males to achieve erections, and the production of male traits in female users.

Anabolic steroids are sometimes given to animals to stimulate the production of lean meat.

Human Reproduction

34

Learning objectives

In this chapter you will learn about:

1 The male reproductive system

2 Male hormones

3 Male infertility

4 The female reproductive system

5 The menstrual cycle

6 A menstrual disorder

7 Female infertility

8 Copulation

9 Pregnancy

10 Development of the embryo

11 Birth

12 Lactation

13 Birth control

14 In-vitro fertilisation

The male reproductive system

The testes

The testes (singular testis) are formed inside the body but they move out of the body around the time of birth. Their function is to produce sperm, to store sperm and to make the male hormone testosterone.

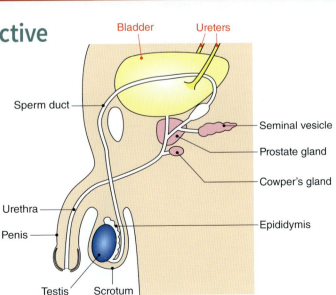

Bladder

Ureters

Sperm duct

Seminal vesicle

Prostate gland

Cowper's gland

Urethra

Epididymis

Penis

Testis

Scrotum

Scrotum

The scrotum maintains the testes at a temperature of 35°C. At this temperature meiosis can take place to form viable sperm. Meiosis will not take place at body temperature (37°C) in males.

Epididymis

The epididymis stores and matures sperm cells.

Sperm ducts

Each sperm duct (or **vas deferens**) transports sperm from the testes to the urethra.

Seminal vesicles, prostate gland and Cowper's gland

These glands produce a fluid called seminal fluid. This fluid causes the sperm to start swimming and provides food for them to swim for about two days.

The combination of sperm and seminal fluid is called **semen**.

Urethra

The urethra is a tube that runs through the middle of the penis. Its functions are to carry sperm (semen) or urine through the penis.

Sperm

Sperm are produced in the testes within a series of tubes. Sperm are produced by meiosis and as a result they are haploid and have only 23 chromosomes.

A *gamete* is a haploid cell capable of fertilisation. Sperm (and eggs) are haploid cells capable of fertilisation, i.e. they are gametes.

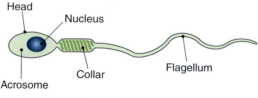

LS of a sperm

Male hormones

Name of hormone	Made in	When made	Functions
FSH (follicle-stimulating hormone)	The pituitary gland	From the onset of sexual maturity (called puberty) until the end of life; puberty takes place around the age of 12 or 13 in males	Stimulates meiosis; as a result it causes sperm to be produced
LH (luteinising hormone)	The pituitary gland	From puberty until the end of life	Stimulates the production of male hormone, testosterone
Testosterone	The testes	From puberty until the end of life	• Initially triggers the formation of the primary male traits • At puberty it causes the secondary male traits

Points to note

Primary male traits include the growth of the male sex organs and the movement of the testes out of the body cavity. **Secondary sexual traits** are traits that distinguish males from females, apart from the sex organs themselves.

Secondary male traits include:

• Growth of body hair
• Growth of larynx (voice box), which causes the voice to deepen
• Growth of muscle and bone
• General body growth
• Increased production of sebum.

Male infertility

Infertility is the inability to produce offspring.

Cause

Low sperm count may be due to one or more of the following: persistent smoking of cigarettes, alcohol abuse, use of marijuana or anabolic steroids or lack of FSH.

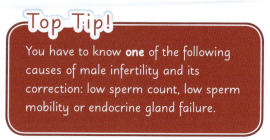

Top Tip!

You have to know **one** of the following causes of male infertility and its correction: low sperm count, low sperm mobility or endocrine gland failure.

Treatment

Depending on the cause, the treatment may involve stopping taking cigarettes, alcohol, marijuana or steroids. Sometimes FSH may be injected. If all of these fail, in-vitro fertilisation may be tried.

The female reproductive system

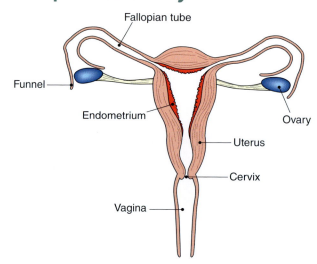

The female reproductive system

The ovaries

At birth, the ovaries contain a large number of potential eggs. From puberty (about 11 years) until the menopause or change of life (between 45 and 55 years) the ovaries normally produce one egg each month. They also produce the female hormones oestrogen and progesterone. Each egg (or ovum) is produced as a result of meiosis. As a result an egg is haploid and contains 23 chromosomes. The egg develops in the ovary inside a fluid-filled sac called the **Graafian follicle**.

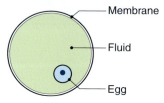

A Graafian follicle

- The Graafian follicle forms the hormone oestrogen during the first half of the menstrual cycle.
- When the Graafian follicle is mature, it moves to the surface of the ovary. At ovulation (in the middle of the menstrual cycle) the Graafian follicle bursts to release an egg.
- The Graafian follicle then enlarges, moves back into the ovary and becomes filled with yellow cells. This yellow structure is then called the corpus luteum or yellow body. The corpus luteum forms the hormone progesterone during the second half of the menstrual cycle.

The Fallopian tube

The funnel of the Fallopian tube collects the egg when it is released from the ovary. The Fallopian tube contains cilia (which are also present in the funnel). The cilia move the egg along the Fallopian tube towards the uterus. The egg may be fertilised in the Fallopian tube (if this does not happen, the egg dies after about 2 days).

Uterus

The uterus (or womb) is the site where the embryo or foetus is nourished during pregnancy. The wall of the uterus is made of involuntary muscle.

The lining of the uterus is called the **endometrium**. This is a soft, spongy tissue that helps to nourish the embryo.

The cervix

The neck of the uterus is called the cervix. This is the opening through which sperm may enter and out through which the baby is born.

The vagina

The vagina is a muscular tube in which sperm are placed during intercourse. It is also the route by which the baby is born.

The menstrual cycle

The menstrual cycle is a series of events that occur every 28 days on average in the female (*mensis* is the Latin word for 'a month'). The menstrual cycle takes place only between puberty and the menopause. It ceases to occur if the female is pregnant.

Events and hormonal control in the menstrual cycle

The menstrual cycle involves four hormones in sequence:

1 FSH   2 oestrogen   3 LH   4 progesterone

Each of these hormones can be said to:

- Cause the production of the next hormone
- Inhibit the production of the preceding hormone.

The role of hormones in the menstrual cycle

Name of hormone	Made in	When made	Functions
FSH (follicle-stimulating hormone)	The pituitary gland	• From puberty to the menopause • Day 1 of each menstrual cycle	• Stimulates meiosis • Causes the production of an egg • Causes the formation of the Graafian follicle
Oestrogen	The Graafian follicle in the ovary	Between days 5 and 14 of the menstrual cycle (very little is made on days 1 to 4 as the Graafian follicle is too small)	• Causes the endometrium to develop • Inhibits FSH (for this reason it is part of the contraceptive pill) • A high level of oestrogen (on day 14) stimulates the release of LH
LH (luteinising hormone)	The pituitary gland	Day 14 of the menstrual cycle	• Causes ovulation (the release of an egg from the ovary) • Causes the Graafian follicle to convert into the corpus luteum • Inhibits the production of oestrogen • Stimulates the production of progesterone
Progesterone	The corpus luteum in the ovary	Day 14 to day 28	• Maintains the growth of the endometrium • Inhibits LH • Prevents the uterus from contracting • Inhibits FSH (along with oestrogen it is part of the contraceptive pill)

Day 28

On day 28 the corpus luteum stops producing progesterone. This results in the following events:

- The uterus can now contract. These contractions cause the endometrium to break down. The blood and tissue are expelled from the body in a process known as **menstruation** (or a period).

- Menstruation marks day 1 of the next cycle and lasts for about 5 days.

- FSH can now be made. It causes a new egg to form on day 1 of the next cycle.

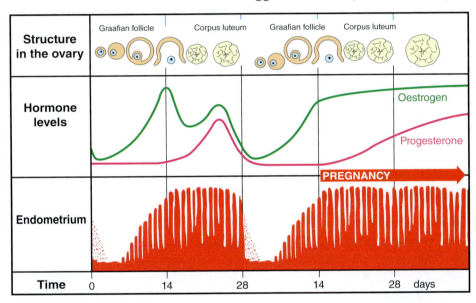

A menstrual disorder

Fibroids

Symptoms

Fibroids are benign tumours of the uterus. They range from the size of a pea to the size of a grapefruit. They are most common in females aged 35 to 45.

Small fibroids produce no symptoms. Larger ones cause severe menstrual bleeding, loss of iron (anaemia), pain, miscarriage or infertility.

Cause

The cause of fibroids is uncertain but they seem to be linked to high levels of oestrogen, i.e. they are more common in those who take the contraceptive pill.

Prevention

Avoidance of oral contraceptives

Treatment

Small fibroids do not require treatment apart from regular observation to see if they have grown. Larger fibroids are removed by surgery.

Female infertility

Endocrine gland failure

Problem

The failure of a female to produce FSH means that she does not produce eggs. Failure to produce LH means that she may make eggs but does not ovulate (this is the most common cause of female infertility).

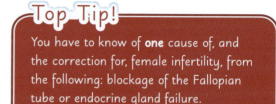

Top Tip!

You have to know of **one** cause of, and the correction for, female infertility, from the following: blockage of the Fallopian tube or endocrine gland failure.

Treatment

The most common treatment involves injecting the appropriate hormone at the correct time in the menstrual cycle. If this fails, in-vitro fertilisation may be attempted.

Copulation

Copulation **means coupling, the act of sexual union or intercourse.**

The stages in copulation include the following:

- Sexual arousal in the male causes blood flow from the penis to become blocked. As a result the penis becomes erect. In females arousal causes the vagina to enlarge and become lubricated. In both genders there is an increase in blood pressure and breathing rates.
- During copulation the penis moves inside the vagina.
- Copulation may result in a series of pleasurable experiences called orgasm. In males, orgasm results in semen being expelled from the penis, a process called **ejaculation**.

Pregnancy

- Sperm are released into the female system in a process called insemination. This takes place in the vagina, close to the cervix.
- The sperm swim towards a chemical released from the egg (this is called chemotaxis).
- The sperm swim through the cervix, along the endometrium and into the Fallopian tube.

- Enzymes from the head (acrosome) of the sperm break down the membrane of the egg.
- The head of the sperm enters the egg (note that the tail, containing mitochondria from the father, remains outside).
- A new (fertilisation) membrane forms around the egg. This prevents any more sperm from entering the egg.

Fertilisation

Fertilisation **is the union of the nuclei of the sperm and egg to form a diploid zygote.**

Fertilisation occurs in the Fallopian tube. It normally takes place on days 14 or 15 of the menstrual cycle.

Fertile time

Eggs can survive for 2 days. Sperm can survive for up to 7 days in the female system.

An egg is normally released on day 14. Fertilisation can occur if sperm enter the female between days 7 and 16 of a normal menstrual cycle. Days 12 to 16 represent the fertile time in the menstrual cycle.

Development of the embryo

- The zygote divides rapidly by mitosis. About 3 days after fertilisation it forms a solid ball of cells called a morula.
- Around day 5, a hollow ball of cells called the **blastocyst** forms.
- The outer cells of the blastocyst (called the trophoblast) will later form the membranes around the embryo.
- The inner cells (called the inner cell mass) will form the embryo.
- The morula is pushed down the Fallopian tube by the movement of cilia.

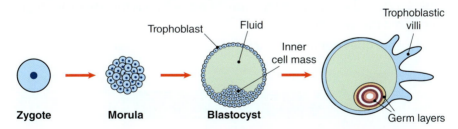

- *Implantation* **is the burrowing of the blastocyst into the lining of the uterus.**
- Implantation normally takes place on day 7 (after fertilisation). At this stage, pregnancy is said to have started.
- The trophoblast forms finger-like projections (villi), which grow into the endometrium. These villi absorb oxygen and food from the blood.

Germ layers

- Around day 10, the inner cell mass becomes arranged to form three original layers of cells (called germ layers). Humans are said to be triploblastic because they arise from three germ layers.

Germ layers **are basic layers of cells in the blastocyst from which all adult tissues and organs will form.**

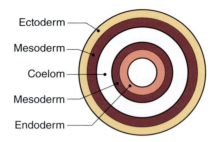

Each of the three germ layers gives rise to different structures in the embryo, as outlined in the following table.

Germ layer	Organ systems formed
Ectoderm	Nervous system, skin, hair and nails
Mesoderm	Muscular, skeletal, circulatory, reproductive and excretory systems
Endoderm	Intestinal lining, lungs, liver and pancreas

The formation of the placenta

- After implantation, the trophoblast forms a membrane called the **amnion** around the developing embryo. Amniotic fluid is formed to protect the embryo.
- The villi formed by the trophoblast grow into the endometrium. The mother's blood vessels grow into the spaces between the villi.
- In this way the placenta starts to form. The placenta is formed by **both** the embryo and the mother.
- The placenta does not become fully functional until about 12 weeks.

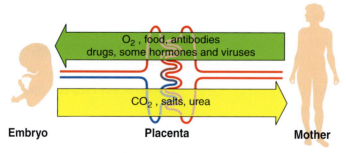

Foetus in the uterus

Functions of the placenta

Exchange

The placenta allows materials to pass from the mother's blood to the embryo and from the embryo's blood to the mother (as shown in the diagram at the bottom of the opposite page).

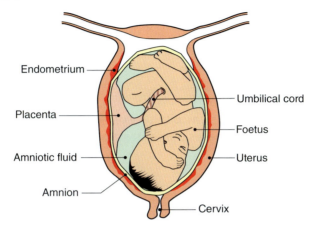

Barrier

The placenta prevents the mother's blood, some hormones and viruses from entering the embryo. The blood vessels of the mother and embryo do not connect in the placenta. This separation is important because:

- They might have different blood groups and the bloods would clump if mixed
- The blood pressure of the mother would be too high for the embryonic tissues.

Endocrine gland

The placenta makes the hormone progesterone from about week 12 of the pregnancy.

Embryonic development up to 3 months

First month	The heart, brain and umbilical cord form.
Week 5	The body organs and limbs start to form.
Week 6	The eyes, ears, mouth and nose form.
Week 8	The body organs have formed. Ovaries or testes have formed. The embryo now looks human and is called a foetus.
Week 12	By the end of the 12th week the placenta is working fully, bones are beginning to replace cartilage, nerves and muscles become coordinated and the baby starts to move its limbs.

Gestation is the length of time the baby spends in the uterus. Gestation lasts 9 months (or 38 weeks) from the time of fertilisation.

Birth

Progesterone

During the pregnancy, progesterone is produced in increasing amounts.

Initially progesterone is produced by the corpus luteum in the ovary, but from about 12 weeks it is produced by the placenta. Progesterone inhibits FSH (and egg production) and inhibits contractions of the uterus. Around the time of the birth, the placenta stops producing progesterone. This allows the uterus to start contracting.

Oxytocin

As the level of progesterone falls, the pituitary of the mother produces the hormone oxytocin. Oxytocin greatly increases the contractions of the uterus walls.

Labour

Contractions of the uterus cause the amnion to burst and the amniotic fluid to be released (the waters are said to break). Soon after this, the baby's head is forced out. The umbilical cord is clamped and cut. A little while later, the afterbirth (consisting of the placenta and the remaining umbilical cord) is expelled from the uterus.

Lactation

Lactation **is the production of milk by the breasts of the female.**

Colostrum

Towards the end of pregnancy the mother produces a liquid called colostrum. This is high in proteins, minerals and antibodies.

Prolactin

The reduction in progesterone around the time of the birth allows the pituitary of the mother to produce the hormone prolactin. Prolactin stimulates the production of milk. Prolactin (and therefore milk) is produced as long as the mother continues to breastfeed the baby.

Benefits of breastfeeding

- Milk contains the ideal balance of nutrients needed for the baby.
- Breast milk supplies antibodies to the baby that prolong its ability to resist infections and reduces the possibility of developing allergies.
- There is less chance of infection from breast milk than if a baby is bottle-fed.
- Breastfeeding helps the mother to lose weight and returns her uterus to the correct shape sooner than bottle-feeding.

- Breastfeeding helps the mother and baby to bond.
- Breastfeeding may help to prevent breast cancer in the mother.

Birth control

- **Birth control** means that steps are taken to limit the number of children that are born.
- ***Contraception* prevents fertilisation or pregnancy.**

There are four categories of contraception: natural, mechanical, chemical and surgical.

Natural contraception

In natural contraception intercourse is avoided on the days immediately before or after ovulation (normally days 12 to 16 of a normal cycle). These methods are about 90% effective.

The methods used to predict the day of ovulation include:

- Recording body temperature (which rises at ovulation)
- Observing changes in the nature of the mucus in the cervix at ovulation
- Predicting the day of ovulation based on previous menstrual cycles (the rhythm method).

Mechanical contraception

Physical barriers are used to prevent sperm from reaching the egg. These methods are about 97% effective.

- A condom is placed over the top of the penis.
- A diaphragm or cap is placed in the vagina and over the cervix.
- A coil (or intra-uterine device, IUD) is placed in the uterus. This prevents implantation.

Chemical contraception

Hormonal methods are about 99% effective.

- The contraceptive pill consists of a combination of oestrogen and progesterone. These hormones prevent eggs from forming. Other, longer-acting hormones can be implanted under the skin.
- Spermicides kill sperm. They are usually used in conjunction with the mechanical methods of contraception.

Surgical contraception

These methods are normally permanent and result in sterilisation. They are generally 100% effective.

- In females the Fallopian tubes are cut and tied in a process called **tubal ligation**. This prevents the sperm from reaching the egg.

- In males the sperm ducts (or vas deferens) are cut and tied in a process called **vasectomy**. This means that there are no sperm present in the semen.

In-vitro fertilisation

In-vitro fertilisation (IVF) is a method of treating male or female infertility.

IVF involves fertilisation outside the body, normally in glass petri dishes (*vitreus* is the Latin word for 'glass').

Process

- Normally the female is given hormones at the start of her cycle to stimulate egg production.
- Around the middle of the cycle, the eggs are removed from the ovary and mixed with sperm in a glass container.
- It is normal for a number of eggs to become fertilised and develop into embryos.
- The embryos may be genetically screened (tested for abnormal genes).
- Some of the embryos are placed in the uterus in the hope that one (or more) of them may become implanted.
- If implantation takes place, the pregnancy follows the normal path. This is why the term 'test-tube baby' is wrong: fertilisation occurs in an artificial manner but the 9 months of pregnancy follow the normal sequence of events in the uterus.

Ethical issue

An ethical issue regarding IVF treatment concerns what to do with the unused embryos that are not placed in the uterus. At present these are frozen for a long time and then destroyed.

Plant Responses

35

Learning objectives

In this chapter you will learn about:

1 Stimulus and response

2 Responses in flowering plants

3 Tropisms

4 Growth regulators

5 Commercial uses of plant growth regulators

6 Auxins (IAA)

7 Plant protective adaptations

Stimulus and response

A *stimulus* is something that causes a reaction (or response) in an organism or in part of an organism.

A *response* is the activity of a cell, organism or part of an organism in reaction to a stimulus.

The ability to respond is often called behaviour and is one of the characteristics of life.

Structures needed for response

The following structures allow organisms to respond:

- A chemical or hormonal system (found in both plants and animals)
- Sense organs and a nervous system (found in animals only)
- The ability to move and grow: plants move slowly by growing in a particular direction, animals move more rapidly because they have muscular and skeletal systems
- An immune system that allows organisms to respond to infection.

Responses in flowering plants

Flowering plants respond to a combination of external and internal factors.

Normally the external factors stimulate the production of internal factors, commonly called growth regulators.

External factors (stimuli)

Flowering plants respond to external factors such as:

- Light intensity (the shoots grow towards light)
- Day length (changes in day length cause flowering, seed and fruit formation, leaf loss, dormancy and seed germination)
- Gravity (shoots grow away from gravity, roots grow towards gravity)
- Temperature (enzymes respond to changes in temperature that in turn affect the rate of growth of plants).

Internal factors (stimuli)

The main internal factors are plant growth regulators. These chemicals are produced in the growing tips (meristems) of the roots and shoots.

Tropisms

A *tropism* is the change in growth of a plant in response to an external stimulus.

- Positive tropisms occur when the plant grows in the direction of the stimulus.
- Negative tropisms occur when the plant grows away from the stimulus.

The advantage of tropisms is that they allow the plant to obtain better growing conditions.

Phototropism

***Phototropism* is the change in growth of a plant in response to light from a given direction.**

- The shoots of a plant are positively phototropic, i.e. they grow towards the light to allow them to get more light and carry out more photosynthesis.
- The roots are negatively phototropic, i.e. they grow away from light to allow them to grow into the soil.

Geotropism

***Geotropism* is the change in growth of a plant in response to gravity.**

- The shoots are negatively geotropic, i.e. they grow away from gravity, which causes them to grow up towards the light.
- The roots are positively geotropic, which causes them to grow down into the soil to improve anchorage and absorption.

Thigmotropism

***Thigmotropism* is the change in growth of a plant in response to touch.**

- Climbing plants such as ivy produce tendrils that respond to touch by growing around the object they touch.

Hydrotropism

Hydrotropism is the change in growth of a plant in response to water in the soil.

- The roots of a plant grow towards damp soil.
- However, roots grow away from waterlogged soil (due to lack of oxygen).

Chemotropism

Chemotropism is the change in growth of a plant in response to chemicals.

- Roots grow towards some chemicals in the soil (e.g. minerals such as calcium and magnesium).
- Roots grow away from toxic chemicals in the soil such as lead and copper.

Growth regulators

Growth regulators are chemicals that control the growth of plants.

Growth regulators are produced in the meristems and carried to their sites of action in the vascular system (i.e. xylem and phloem). This is similar to the way hormones in humans are produced in one location but are carried in the blood to where they act. Growth regulators are often compared to hormones.

It is difficult to identify the precise function of growth regulators for the following reasons:

- They are active in tiny amounts
- They have different effects depending on their concentrations
- They have different effects depending on where they act
- They interact with each other; this means they may increase the effect but they can also cancel each other out to decrease the effect.

Growth inhibitors

Growth inhibitors reduce the growth of plants.

- Abscisic acid (or ABA) inhibits growth in seeds and results in dormancy.
- Ethene is a gas that inhibits growth in petioles and results in leaf fall in autumn.

Growth promoters

Growth promoters increase the growth of plants. IAA is an example of a growth promoter (see overleaf).

Commercial uses of plant growth regulators

- **Rooting powder** (or liquid) often contains an artificially produced growth regulator (such as NAA). Rooting powder is used to stimulate root growth in cuttings.
- **Selective weedkiller** (such as 2, 4-D) will kill dicots (such as weeds) but have no effect on monocots (such as grass or cereal crops).
- **Ethene** is used to cause green bananas to turn yellow (i.e. to ripen them).

Auxins (IAA)

Auxins are a family of growth regulators. The most commonly studied auxin is indoleacetic acid (IAA).

Production sites

Auxins are produced mainly in shoot tip meristems. They may also be produced in young leaves and in developing seeds.

Functions

The functions of auxins include the following:

- They loosen cellulose fibres in cell walls allowing the cell to elongate
- They cause different tissues to form (differentiation)
- They inhibit side branching in stems.

Effects

Auxins cause the following effects:

- **Tropisms** are caused by auxins. (The way in which IAA causes phototropism is described below.)
- **Apical dominance** means that auxins produced in the apical (shoot tip) meristem pass down the stem and inhibit side branches. This allows the plant to grow tall.

If the apical tips are removed (by clipping a hedge, for example), the side branches can form, which allows the hedge to fill out and grow more thickly.

- **Fruit formation** is stimulated by IAA made in developing seeds.

How IAA causes phototropism

- IAA is produced in the shoot tip meristem.
- IAA passes down the stem.
- In normal light, IAA passes down each side of a stem equally. It loosens the cell walls and allows them to expand. If all the cells expand equally, the stem grows straight up.
- When light comes from one side (unidirectional light) IAA passes down the shady side of the stem. Cells on the shady side elongate, but those on the bright side do not elongate.

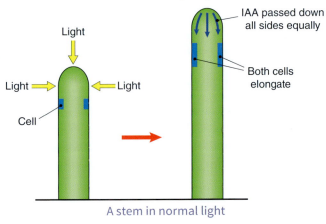

A stem in normal light

- The difference in elongation causes the stem to grow towards the light.

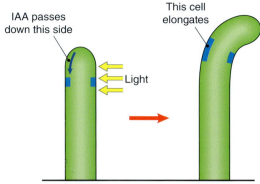

A stem in light from one side

Experiment

To investigate the effect of IAA on plant tissue

Preparing a stock solution of IAA

(Note: The teacher often carries out this preparation (as IAA is slightly carcinogenic) and the stock solution is then used by the class.)

1. Dissolve a small amount of IAA powder in a small volume of ethanol. *(IAA dissolves better in ethanol than it does in water.)*

2. Add the IAA solution to a volumetric flask and make up to 1 litre using distilled water. *(If the correct amounts are used the stock solution contains IAA at a concentration of 100, or 10^2, parts per million (ppm).)*

Preparing different concentrations of IAA

1. Label eight containers A to H.

2. Add some of the prepared stock IAA solution to dish A using a pipette.

3. Add equal volumes of water to dishes B to H, but do not add any water to dish A.

4. Use a pipette or a syringe to transfer some of the IAA solution from dish A into dish B and mix well.

5. Use a pipette to transfer the same volume of IAA solution from dish B to C and mix well.

6. Repeat the previous step, transferring the same volume of liquid each time from C to D, D to E, E to F and F to G. *(The process carried out at points 2 to 6 is called a serial dilution. It produces concentrations that are increasingly dilute, i.e. the solutions are 100 (10^2) ppm, 10 (10^1) ppm, 1(10^0) ppm, 0.1(10^{-1}) ppm, 0.01 (10^{-2}) ppm, 0.001 (10^{-3}) ppm and 0.0001(10^{-4}) ppm, respectively.)*

7. Remove the same volume of solution from dish G and dispose of it. *(This means that dish H has no IAA and acts as a control.)*

8. Each dish now has an equal volume of liquid.

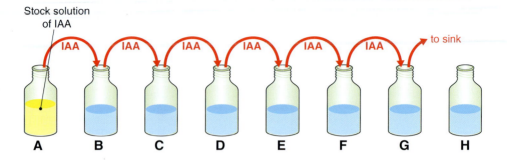

Stock solution of IAA

IAA → IAA → IAA → IAA → IAA → IAA → to sink

A B C D E F G H

Testing the effects of IAA on plant tissue

1. Place a disc of graphed acetate paper in the lid of a petri dish. (*The graph lines on the acetate allow you to measure the length of the stems or roots.*)

2. Place five radish (or cress) seeds along one of the lines on the acetate.

3. Place a sheet of filter paper over the seeds.

4. Use a clean dropper or pipette to wet the filter paper with some of the prepared solution from dish A.

5. Cover the filter paper with cotton wool.

6. Pour the remains of the solution from dish A onto the cotton wool.

7. Place the base on the petri dish and tape it shut.

8. Repeat this procedure for each of the solutions B to H. (The petri dishes are labelled 10^2, 10^1, 10^0, 10^{-1}, 10^{-2}, 10^{-3}, 10^{-4} and control, respectively.)

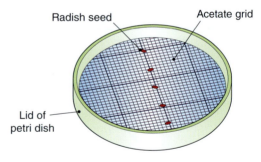

Radish seed
Acetate grid
Lid of petri dish

9. Place the petri dishes standing on their sides in a warm room or in an incubator at 25°C for 3 to 7 days. (*Standing the dishes on their sides allows the shoots to grow straight up and the roots to grow straight down. If the dishes are placed in the wrong positions, the shoots and roots may grow on top of each other and it is hard to measure their lengths.*)

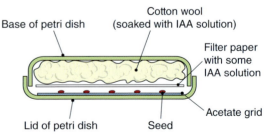

Base of petri dish
Cotton wool (soaked with IAA solution)
Filter paper with some IAA solution
Lid of petri dish
Seed
Acetate grid

Results

1. After a few days, measure the lengths of the roots and shoots of all the seedlings and calculate the averages.

2. Calculate the percentage stimulation (elongation) or inhibition (contraction) for the roots and/or the shoots in each dish according to the formula:

$$\frac{(\text{Average length} - \text{average length of control}) \times 100}{\text{Average length of control}}$$

3. The typical results are that depending on the IAA concentration used:

   - The roots may grow longer or shorter than those in the control (or there may be no root growth)
   - The shoots may grow longer or shorter than those in the control (or there may be no shoot growth).

Plant protective adaptations

Structural features

- Epidermis cells are closely packed to reduce water loss and prevent the entry of pathogens. The cuticle helps in both of these functions.
- Other protective features include stinging hairs on nettles and sharp thorns on roses.

Chemical features

- Plants produce a variety of chemicals to prevent them from being eaten. For example, oaks produce tannins in their leaves.
- Heat-shock proteins are produced during high temperatures to prevent plant enzymes from losing shape.

36 The Skeleton and Muscles

Functions of the skeleton

- **Support:** The skeleton supports the body and keeps it upright.
- **Shape:** The skeleton gives shape to the body.
- **Protection:** The skull protects the brain, the backbone protects the spinal cord and the ribs protect the lungs.
- **Movement:** The bones of the skeleton provide rigid levers against which the muscles can pull.
- **Manufacture of blood cells:** Red cells, white cells and platelets are made in the bone marrow of the long bones in the skeleton.

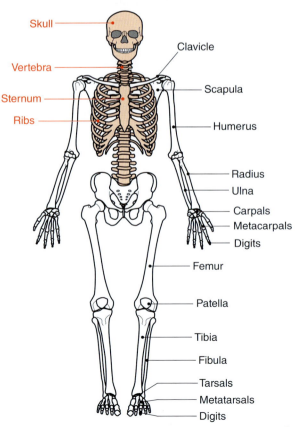

THE AXIAL SKELETON   **THE APPENDICULAR SKELETON**

Skull

Clavicle

Vertebra

Scapula

Sternum

Ribs

Humerus

Radius

Ulna

Carpals

Metacarpals

Digits

Femur

Patella

Tibia

Fibula

Tarsals

Metatarsals

Digits

A human skeleton

The axial skeleton

The *axial skeleton* consists of the skull, vertebrae, ribs and sternum.

Skull

The skull consists of 22 bones, most of which are fused together to form the cranium.

Spine

The spine contains 33 bones called vertebrae. The vertebrae surround and protect the nerves of the spinal cord.

A pad of fluid enclosed by cartilage, called a disc, is located between most of the vertebrae. These discs act as shock absorbers and protect the vertebrae from rubbing against each other. The vertebrae are arranged as follows:

Region	Number of vertebrae
Cervical (or neck)	7
Thoracic (or chest)	12
Lumbar (or small of back)	5
Sacrum (or hip)	5
Coccyx (or tail)	4

Ribs

We have twelve pairs of ribs. All of the ribs are attached to the spine. There are three types of ribs, depending on what they attach to at the front of the body.

Type	Number of ribs (pairs)	Attachment at front
True ribs	7	Sternum
False ribs	3	Rib above
Floating ribs	2	None

The appendicular skeleton

The *appendicular skeleton* consists of the pectoral and pelvic girdles, along with their attached limbs (the arms and legs).

Pectoral girdle

- The pectoral girdle contains the clavicles (or collar bones) and the scapulae (or shoulder blades).
- The arms consist of the humerus, the radius, the ulna, the carpals (or bones of the wrist), the metacarpals (or bones of the hand) and five digits or fingers (which are composed of bones called phalanges).

Pelvic girdle

- The pelvic girdle contains the hip bones, which are attached to the sacrum. The hip bones surround a hollow cavity called the pelvis.
- The legs consist of the femur (or thigh bone, the longest and largest bone in the body), the patella (or knee cap), the tibia (or shin bone), the fibula (a small bone parallel to the shin bone), the tarsals (bones of the ankle), the metatarsals (or bones of the foot) and five digits or toes (which are composed of bones called phalanges).

Structure of a long bone

Compact bone

Compact bone is composed of bone cells called osteoblasts enclosed in a matrix. The matrix consists of 70% inorganic salts (such as calcium carbonate and phosphate) and 30% organic material (such as the protein collagen). The inorganic material gives **strength** to the bone. The organic material gives the bone its **flexibility**. Compact bone also contains blood vessels and nerve fibres.

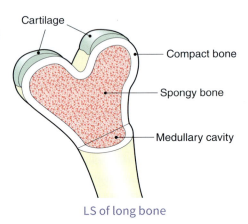

LS of long bone

Medullary cavity

The medullary cavity contains a soft material called bone marrow.

- Red marrow is active in making blood cells.
- Yellow marrow is inactive and contains numerous fat-storage cells. It can convert to active red marrow if required.

Spongy bone

Spongy bone consists of a mixture of compact bone with pockets of bone marrow. Its function is to give strength and rigidity to bones without making them too heavy.

Cartilage

Cartilage is a flexible material that consists of protein fibres embedded in a rubbery matrix. Cartilage protects the ends of long bones and acts as a shock absorber.

Bone growth

Initial bone growth

Initially the skeleton of an embryo is made of cartilage. From about 8 weeks into its development the cartilage of the embryo is replaced by bone. This process is called ossification. Bone-forming cells are called **osteoblasts**. When the osteoblasts become trapped in the newly formed bone matrix they form dormant cells. The increase in length of a bone is caused by a section of cartilage called the growth plate. Growth plates are found between each medullary cavity and the spongy bone.

In the growth plate, osteoblasts form bone matrix (mostly calcium phosphate) to extend the length of the bone. Growth plates cease to function at about 16 in females and at about 18 in males.

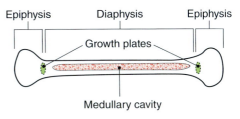

Growth plates in a long bone

Bone development

- Bone is continually dissolved and replaced (about ten times) during life. Catabolic, bone-digesting cells remove calcium from the inside of the medullary cavity. They deposit this calcium in blood vessels. This prevents bone from becoming too heavy.

- At the same time, anabolic, bone-forming cells (osteoblasts) form new bone. Physical activity, hormones and diet influence the coordination of the two types of bone cell.
  - Physical activity stimulates the osteoblasts. This results in stronger bones.
  - Human growth hormone and sex hormones (testosterone, oestrogen and progesterone) increase the size and strength of bones. This is seen by the increased growth at puberty when these hormones are produced in large amounts. In addition, females often suffer from a loss of bone strength after the menopause due to the reduced levels of their sex hormones.
  - It is important to have sufficient levels of calcium in the diet to allow proper bone growth. This is especially true at puberty, but is also important in later years as bone is continually broken down.

Ligaments

Ligaments **connect bone to bone.** Ligaments are made of strong, slightly elastic fibres.

Tendons

Tendons **connect muscle to bone.** Tendons are made of strong, flexible, non-elastic fibres.

Joints

A *joint* **is where two or more bones meet.** Joints may be classified into three groups according to the range of movement they allow.

Immovable joints

- Immovable joints allow no movement between the bones. Their function is strength and protection.
- Examples include the skull and coccyx.

Slightly movable joints

- Slightly movable joints allow a small amount of movement between the bones.
- Examples are the joints between the vertebrae in the spinal cord. This movement allows the spinal column to have some flexibility without damaging the nerves of the spinal cord, which run through the vertebrae.

Freely movable joints

Freely movable joints have cartilage covering the ends of the bones and have a gap between the bones. They are also called synovial joints.

Synovial fluid is found in the gap between the bones. This fluid helps to lubricate the joint. There are two main types of synovial joints:

- **Ball and socket**, e.g. the shoulders and hip. These joints allow movement in all directions.
- **Hinge**, e.g. the elbow and knee. These joints allow movement in one direction only.

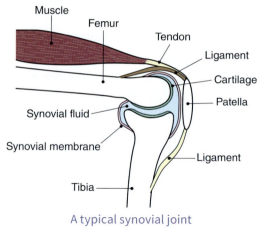

Typical synovial joint

The knee is an example of a typical synovial joint.

A typical synovial joint

Disorder of the musculoskeletal system

Arthritis

Cause

Arthritis (of which there are over 100 different types) is caused by swelling of the joints.

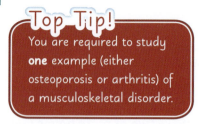

Top Tip!
You are required to study **one** example (either osteoporosis or arthritis) of a musculoskeletal disorder.

- Osteoarthritis is caused by wear and tear to cartilage in the joint. It usually affects one or a few joints.
- Rheumatoid arthritis is caused by the body's immune system attacking its own joints. It affects most of the joints in the body.

Prevention

Reducing wear and tear on specific joints may prevent osteoarthritis. For example, athletes should wear proper footwear and switch to non-impact exercise (such as swimming) if a joint becomes sore and inflamed.

Treatment

Arthritis is normally incurable. Treatment includes rest, weight loss, special exercises to maintain agility, anti-inflammatory medication and, in severe cases, surgery to repair the damage.

Muscles

Muscles are made of protein. There are three types of muscle:

- Involuntary (smooth) muscle is located in the intestines, blood vessels and bladder.
- Cardiac muscle is located in the heart.
- Voluntary (skeletal or striped) muscle is the muscle that causes body movements. These muscles work as antagonistic pairs.

Antagonistic pairs

Muscles can only contract (i.e. they cannot make themselves elongate). This means that a second muscle is required to elongate the first muscle. Muscles work in pairs.

An *antagonistic* pair consists of two muscles that have opposite effects.

For example, the biceps and triceps in the upper arm form an antagonistic pair.

- The triceps contracts (while the biceps relaxes) to lower the forearm.
- The biceps contracts (while the triceps relaxes) to raise the forearm.

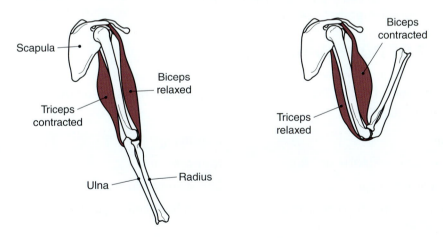

The action of an antagonistic pair

37 Viruses

Learning objectives

In this chapter you will learn about:

1 The structure of viruses

2 Living or non-living?

3 Shapes of viruses

4 Virus replication

5 Medical and economic importance of viruses

6 Control of virus infections

The structure of viruses

Viruses are tiny structures that can be viewed only using an electron microscope.

They consist of an outer protein coat and a strand of nucleic acid, either DNA or RNA.

Viruses are not cells as they do not have membranes or any cell organelles. They do not carry out normal metabolic reactions.

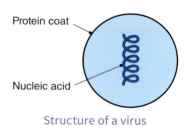

Structure of a virus

Living or non-living?

Viruses are not included in any of the five kingdoms of living things. This is because viruses do not exhibit all the features of a living thing. Viruses are on the border between living and non-living.

Living	Non-living
Have nucleic acid (DNA or RNA)	Non-cellular
Have a protein coat	Cannot reproduce by themselves
Can replicate and pass on genetic information	Do not have cell organelles
	Have only one type of nucleic acid (i.e. they have DNA or RNA; living things have both)
	Do not feed or respire

Shapes of viruses

Viruses may have three distinct shapes:

- Rod-shaped, e.g. tobacco mosaic virus
- Round or polyhedral, e.g. influenza or mumps
- Complex, e.g. the T phage (a virus that infects bacteria).

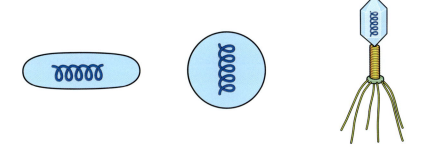

Virus replication

Viruses enter a host cell and use the energy and organelles of the host to produce new viruses. For this reason viruses are said to be **obligate parasites**. Viruses cannot be grown on agar; they can grow only inside a live host. Viruses do not reproduce themselves; they are said to replicate.

Process

- A virus lands on a host cell.
- The DNA of the virus enters the host while the protein coat stays outside or is digested if it enters.
- Sometimes the virus DNA joins with the host DNA (or chromosome) but sometimes it stays separate. If the virus has RNA this is converted by the host cell into DNA.
- The DNA of the virus causes the host cell to produce new virus coats and new virus DNA. New viruses are assembled in the host cell.
- The host cell bursts to release new virus particles.

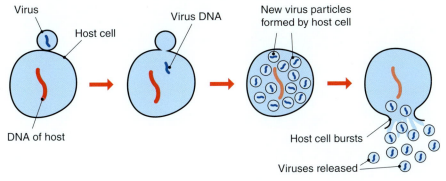

Virus replication

Medical and economic importance of viruses

Disadvantages of viruses

- Viruses cause human diseases such as colds, influenzas (flu), measles, mumps, chicken pox, polio, rabies, cold sores and AIDS.
  Human diseases cause medical problems. They also result in economic losses such as medical costs and lost time at work.
- Viruses cause animal diseases such as foot and mouth in cattle and rabies in dogs.
- Viruses cause plant diseases such as tobacco, tomato and potato mosaic diseases.

Benefits of viruses

- They are sometimes used to transfer genes from one organism to another in genetic engineering.
- They provide restriction enzymes, which are used to cut DNA in genetic engineering and when producing DNA profiles.
- There is hope that bacteriophages (viruses that infect and destroy bacteria) may be used to control some bacterial infections.

Control of virus infections

- Viruses are controlled by the body's general defence system (i.e. skin, stomach acid, phagocytes, etc.) and by the specific defence system (i.e. we produce antibodies against viruses).
- Vaccinations are available for some viral diseases (e.g. the MMR vaccination prevents measles, mumps and rubella).
- Antibiotics do **not** affect viruses.
- Drugs such as interferon and acyclovir have been developed to interfere with viral replication.

Sexual Reproduction in Flowering Plants

38

Learning objectives

In this chapter you will learn about:

1. The structure of a flower
2. Formation of male gametes
3. Formation of female gametes
4. Pollination
5. Fertilisation
6. Seed formation
7. Dispersal
8. Dormancy
9. Germination

The structure of a flower

Receptacle

The receptacle is a swelling at the base of the flower. It supports the flower.

Sepals

The function of the sepals is to protect the flower when it is a bud.

Petals

The function of the petals is to protect the other parts of the flower. In some cases they attract insects.

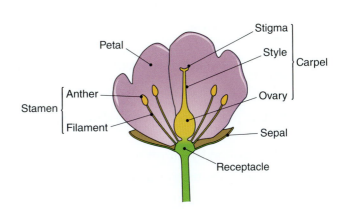

Stamens

The stamens are the male part of the flower. The anther produces pollen grains (as a result of meiosis). The filament supports the anther.

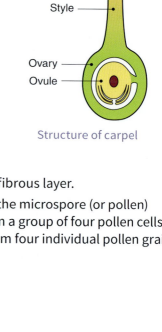

Structure of stamen

Carpels

The carpels are the female part of the flower.

- The stigma is the place where pollen grains land.
- The style connects the stigma to the ovary.
- The ovary contains one or more ovules. Each ovule produces an egg (as a result of meiosis).

Structure of carpel

Formation of male gametes

- Each anther is composed of four chambers called pollen sacs.
- Each pollen sac is lined with an epidermis and a fibrous layer.
- Each pollen sac has a layer of diploid cells called the microspore (or pollen) mother cells. These cells divide by meiosis to form a group of four pollen cells called a tetrad. The tetrad soon splits apart to form four individual pollen grains.

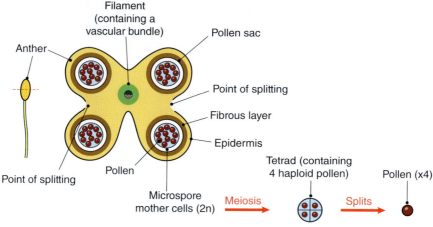

Pollen formation

- The immature pollen grains are called microspores. Each pollen grain has a single haploid nucleus.
- This nucleus divides by mitosis to form two haploid nuclei.
  - One of these (the tube nucleus) does not divide any more.
  - The second nucleus (the generative nucleus) divides by mitosis to form two sperm nuclei. These nuclei are the male gametes.
- The mature pollen grain forms a tough, patterned outer wall called the exine. The inner, flexible wall of the pollen grain is called the intine.

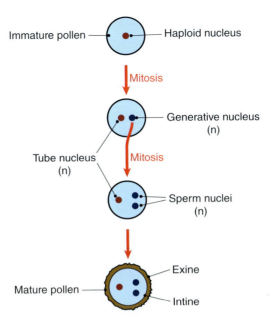

- Pollen grains are formed **inside** the anther. When the pollen grains are mature, the anther breaks open and the walls of the pollen sacs fold back.
- This means that the pollen grains are exposed on the **outside** of the anther.

Formation of female gametes

- Each ovule has two walls called integuments. There is a small opening in the integuments called the micropyle. This allows the pollen tube to enter the ovule.
- The bulk of the ovule consists of diploid nourishing cells called the nucellus.
- The megaspore mother cell (or embryo sac mother cell) is a single diploid cell in the centre of the ovule.

  This cell divides by meiosis to form the embryo sac, which contains four haploid nuclei.

  — Three of these nuclei die.

  — The fourth nucleus divides by mitosis three times to form eight haploid nuclei.

- One of these nuclei becomes the egg nucleus, which forms the egg cell.

  Two more form the polar nuclei. (The other five nuclei die and play no part in reproduction).

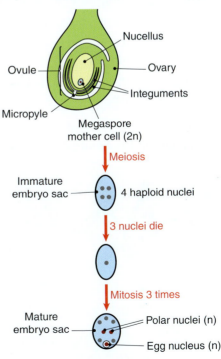

Formation of female gametes

- The egg cell and the two polar nuclei are the female gametes.
- The carpel now appears as shown in the diagram.

Pollination

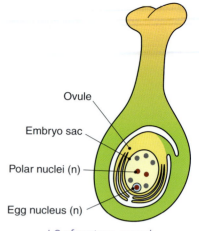

LS of mature carpel

Pollination is the transfer of pollen from an anther to a carpel.

- *Self-pollination* means that the anther and carpel are on the same plant.

  Self-pollination leads to self-fertilisation, which in turn produces offspring that are weaker. Self-pollination occurs in cereals.

- *Cross-pollination* means that the anther and carpel are on different plants.

  Cross-pollination leads to cross-fertilisation, which produces stronger and healthier offspring.

Methods of cross-pollination

	Wind	Animal
Petals	Small, green, no scent or nectar	Large, brightly coloured, scent and nectar
Pollen	Huge amounts, small, light	Smaller amounts, large, sticky
Anthers	Large, outside petals	Smaller, inside petals
Stigmas	Large and feathery, outside petals	Smaller, rounded, inside petals
Example	Grasses, conifers, oak, alder	Orchids, daisies, dandelions, buttercups

Hay fever is caused by a reaction to pollen grains. This reaction is most likely to be triggered by wind-pollinated plants (as they produce most pollen).

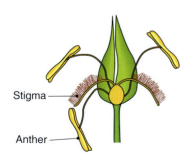

Wind-pollinated flower

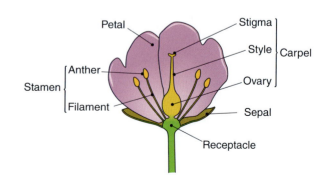

Insect-pollinated flower

Fertilisation

***Fertilisation* is the union of the male and female gametes.**

When the pollen grain lands on the stigma it forms a pollen tube. The tube nucleus causes the pollen tube to grow down through the style and into the ovule at the micropyle. The tube nucleus then dies.

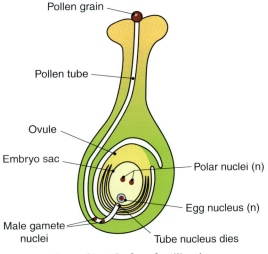

Carpel just before fertilisation

Double fertilisation

- One of the male gamete nuclei joins with the egg nucleus to form a diploid zygote.
- The second male gamete nucleus joins with the two polar nuclei to form a triploid endosperm.

Seed formation

- After fertilisation the ovule becomes a seed.
- The triploid endosperm grows rapidly and absorbs the nucellus.
- The zygote grows by mitosis to form the embryo (which is the new plant).
- The embryo consists of a plumule (which will form the future shoots of the plant) and a radicle (which will give rise to the future roots).
- As the embryo grows inside the seed, it produces one or two seed leaves or cotyledons. The cotyledons are diploid and absorb the endosperm to act as a food store in the seed.
- The walls of the ovule (integuments) become the seed coat (or testa).

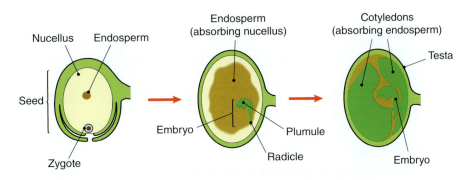

Development of seed after fertilisation

Types of seed

Number of cotyledons

Plants that form a seed with a single seed leaf or cotyledon are called monocots, while plants with two cotyledons in each seed are called dicots.

Presence/absence of endosperm

In monocots the cotyledon absorbs food from the endosperm and normally passes it on to the embryo (i.e. the cotyledons do not normally store food). This means that, at maturity, monocot seeds (such as grasses, cereals and maize) generally have some endosperm. They are said to be endospermic.

In dicots the cotyledons absorb food from the endosperm and act as food stores.

This means that dicot seeds generally do not have an endosperm at maturity. They are said to be non-endospermic.

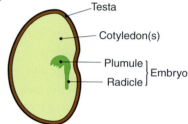

A dicot seed (broad bean)

Fruit

- The developing seeds produce growth regulators, such as auxins. These regulators stimulate the formation of fruits.
- A fruit normally forms from the ovary. The fruit encloses the seed or seeds.
- Fruits protect the seeds and may help to disperse them.
  - Some fruits are dry, e.g. grass and cereal grains, bean and pea pods.
  - Many fruits are moist and edible, e.g. tomatoes, grapes and oranges.

Seedless fruit

The formation of fruit without a seed is called parthenocarpy. It is a form of virgin birth (i.e. there is no fertilisation).

Examples of seedless fruits are bananas, grapes, oranges and pineapples.

- Some seedless fruits occur naturally
- Seedless fruits may be produced commercially in two ways
  - Special breeding programmes have produced large seedless fruits and vegetables.
  - Spraying plants with growth regulators (such as auxin) stimulates them to produce seedless fruit.

Dispersal

Dispersal is the carrying of the seed as far as possible from the parent plant.

The benefits of dispersal

- To reduce competition
- To increase the chances of survival

- To find new areas for growth
- To increase the numbers of the species.

Methods of dispersal

Wind dispersal

- Some seeds (e.g. orchids) are very small and are blown long distances by the wind.
- Dandelions have a feathery parachute to carry a larger seed.
- Sycamore and ash have winged fruits to help the wind blow the seeds further.

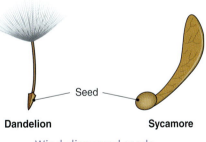

Dandelion   Seed   Sycamore

Wind-dispersed seeds

Water dispersal

- Plants such as water lily, alder and coconuts have light, air-filled fruits that can float and are dispersed by water.

Animal dispersal

There are two main types of animal-dispersed seeds.

- Sticky fruits attach to the animal and fall off some time later. Examples include burdock, goose grass and buttercup.
- Edible fruits such as blackberries, raspberries and strawberries are eaten and digested by animals. However, the seeds are not digested and pass out of the animals' intestines some time (and place) later.

Self-dispersal

- Plants such as peas and beans have dry fruits called pods. These pods shrivel and burst to expel the seeds.

Dormancy

Dormancy is a resting period when seeds undergo no growth and have reduced cell activity or metabolism.

Most seeds do not grow or germinate as soon as they are formed. They go through a resting period called dormancy. Very often the seeds will not germinate until the following spring.

Causes of dormancy

- Growth inhibitors (e.g. abscisic acid) may be present in the testa. These prevent the embryo from growing. Growth inhibitors may be removed by water, cold temperatures or decay.
- The testa may be impermeable to water or oxygen, which can enter only when the testa decays.
- The testa may be too tough for the embryo to penetrate it.
- Growth promoters may take time to be produced. This often happens in spring.

Advantages of dormancy

- Allows time for seed dispersal
- Allows a long growing season for seedlings
- Helps the seedling to avoid the harsh conditions of winter
- Different lengths of dormancy mean that there are always some seeds in the soil (this helps the species to survive).

Agricultural and horticultural practices associated with dormancy

Dormancy means that seeds remain viable (i.e. capable of growing into new plants) for long periods of time, often more than a year. This allows seeds to be stored and sold in packets.

Before planting, it may be necessary to treat the seeds in order to break their dormancy. This may involve:

- Soaking the seeds in water
- Placing them in a cold place overnight
- Scraping their surface to break the tough testa.

Germination

Germination is the re-growth of the embryo into a new plant.

Conditions needed for germination

- **Water** is needed to allow enzyme action
- **Oxygen** is needed to allow respiration
- A **suitable temperature** is needed to allow enzyme action to proceed.

(In addition, dormancy must be completed).

Events in germination

- The seed absorbs water, swells and the testa bursts.
- Enzymes in the seed become active. These enzymes digest food stored in the seed to provide the raw materials for the growth of the embryo.

For example:

$$Starch \xrightarrow{amylase} Maltose$$

$$Fats \xrightarrow{lipase} Fatty\ acids + glycerol$$

$$Proteins \xrightarrow{proteases} Amino\ acids$$

- The embryo absorbs the products of digestion. This means that the mass (weight) of the embryo increases.
- The mass of the food stores (the cotyledons and/or the endosperm) in the seed falls.
- The overall dry mass of the seed falls due to energy losses in respiration.
- The radicle bursts through the testa.
- The hypocotyl (the area between the radicle and the point of attachment to the cotyledon) grows, causing the radicle to grow down into the soil.
- The plumule emerges from the seed.
- If the epicotyl (the area between the plumule and the point of attachment to the cotyledon) grows, the plumule will grow upwards and out of the soil.
- The radicle develops into the root system.
- The plumule forms the first true leaves.

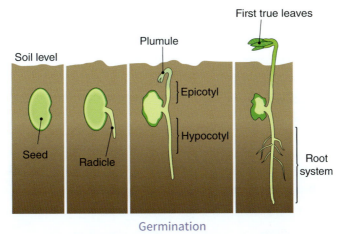

Germination

In the previous diagram the cotyledons stay below the soil during germination. In the following diagram the cotyledons are pulled up out of the soil.

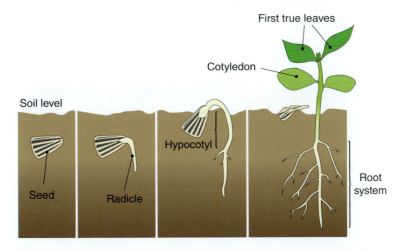

To investigate the effects of water, oxygen and temperature on germination

1. Place filter paper or cotton wool in the base of four petri dishes.

2. Add water to the filter paper in dishes A, C and D.

3. Place five seeds in each petri dish.

4. Dish C is placed in a refrigerator at 4°C. Dishes A, B and D are left at room temperature (20°C).

5. Dish D is placed in a jar that contains anaerobic conditions. Anaerobic conditions are created by using an anaerobic kit that absorbs oxygen. *(Dish A is the control as it has all three factors, dish B has no water, dish C has an unsuitable temperature and dish D has no oxygen.)*

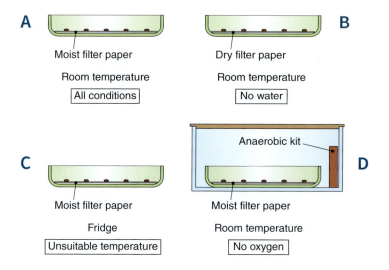

6. The dishes are left in place for a few days.

7. The results (and the reasons for them) are shown in the table below.

8. This shows that seeds need water, oxygen and a suitable temperature to germinate.

Tube	Factors present	Factors absent	Result
A	Water, O_2 + suitable temperature	None	Germination
B	O_2 + suitable temperature	Water	No germination
C	Water + O_2	Suitable temperature	No germination
D	Water + suitable temperature	O_2	No germination

To show digestive action during germination

1 Soak some seeds (maize, barley or broad beans) in water overnight.

2 Wash the bench with mild disinfectant solution. *(This kills any micro-organisms on the bench.)*

3 Boil half of the seeds in water for 5 minutes. *(This will kill them and allow them to be used as a control.)*

4 Split the seeds in half (using a backed blade).

5 Soak all the half-seeds in mild disinfectant solution. *(This sterilises them and prevents the growth of micro-organisms.)*

6 Flame a forceps. *(This sterilises it.)*

7 Using the flamed forceps place two halves of an unboiled seed face down on starch agar in a petri dish. *(This allows the enzymes in the seed to come into contact with the starch in the agar.)*

8 Place two halves of a boiled seed face down on starch agar on the other side of the petri dish *(as a control).*

9 Cover the dish, label it and leave in a warm place for a few days. *(This gives the enzymes time to digest the starch in the agar.)*

10 After a few days remove the seeds and pour dilute iodine solution over the surface of the agar. *(Iodine tests for the presence of starch.)*

11 The results are as follows:

- Boiled seeds

  The agar in the part of the dish with the boiled seeds turns blue-black.

- Unboiled seeds

  The agar around the unboiled seeds turns blue-black.

The agar under the unboiled seeds remains clear. *(The starch was not broken down as boiling denatured the enzymes.)*

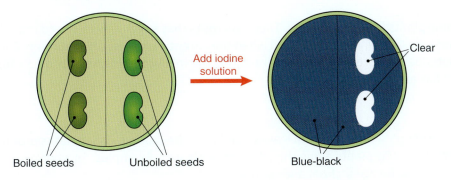

Boiled seeds   Unboiled seeds   Add iodine solution   Clear   Blue-black

39 Vegetative Propagation

Learning objectives

In this chapter you will learn about:

1 Vegetative propagation
2 Natural methods of vegetative propagation
3 Artificial methods of vegetative propagation
4 Comparing sexual and vegetative propagation

Vegetative propagation

Vegetative propagation (or vegetative reproduction) means asexual reproduction in plants.

In vegetative propagation, part of the parent plant becomes detached and grows to form a new plant. Plants produced as a result of vegetative propagation are genetically identical to the parent plant.

Natural methods of vegetative propagation

Stem

Runners are stems that grow over-ground from the parent plant. When the runner is far enough from the parent, it produces roots and stems to form a new plant. Examples: strawberries and buttercups.

Root

Some plants form root tubers. These are roots that swell up with stored food. The root tubers survive underground when the parent plant dies off in autumn. Each root tuber can produce a new plant during the following growing season. Examples: dahlias and sweet potatoes.

Leaf

Some plants reproduce from leaves that fall to the ground. Other plants produce numerous new plants along the edge of their leaves. Examples: 'mother-of-thousands' (or Kalanchoe) and cactus.

Bulbs

Bulbs contain many buds. New plants can be formed from the buds that are located between the swollen, fleshy leaves of the bulb. Examples: onions, daffodils and tulips.

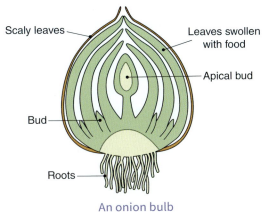

Scaly leaves

Leaves swollen with food

Apical bud

Bud

Roots

An onion bulb

Artificial methods of vegetative propagation

Cuttings

A cutting is a part of a shoot that is removed from the parent plant. The cutting may be planted directly in soil or placed in water for roots to form. Very often, rooting hormone is applied to the end of the cutting to speed up root formation. Examples: busy Lizzie and geraniums.

Grafting

Grafting involves attaching a section of one plant (called the scion) into a cut in a second plant (the stock). The process is successful if the two growing regions (called meristems) merge together. Examples: apple and cherry trees.

Layering

Layering involves bending a long stem over so that part of it can be attached to the soil. A new plant forms where the stem meets the soil. Examples: blackberries and roses.

Micropropagation

Micropropagation is also called tissue culture. In this process, cells are extracted from the parent plant and grown in a liquid culture or on agar. The cells form a mass of undifferentiated cells called a callus. Given the correct conditions and growth regulators, each callus will form a new plant. This method allows huge numbers of plants to be formed from one desired plant. Examples: orchids, bananas and potatoes.

Comparing sexual and vegetative propagation

The advantages and disadvantages of plant sexual and non-sexual (vegetative) reproduction are outlined in the following table.

Sexual reproduction (seeds)	Vegetative propagation
Advantages	
Offspring show variations	Offspring are identical
Less competition due to dispersal	Simple process
Variations allow for disease resistance	No external agents
Disadvantages	
Complex process	No variation (i.e. evolution is slower)
Depends on external agents	Danger of overcrowding and competition
Wasteful of flowering parts such as petals, nectar, pollen, seeds and fruit	All plants may be affected by the same disease

INDEX

A

abiotic factors   13, 31–2

acquired variations   77

adrenal glands   185

alcohol fermentation   63

alimentary canal   152

alleles   78

alveoli   166–7

Amoeba   121

anabolic steroids   186

anabolism   11

animal

    cells   36

    tissues   41

antibiotic resistance   115

antibiotics   115

antibodies   136–7

antigens   136–7

aquatic factors   14

arteries   142

arthritis   212–13

asthma   168–9

auxins (IAA)   204–7

B

bacteria   107, 109–115

B-cells   138

bile   155

bioprocessing   64–5

biosphere, definition   12

biotic factors   13

birth   198

    control   199

blood   131–4

    groups   134

    pressure   148

    vessels   142–3

bone

    growth   210–11

    structure   210

brain   173

breastfeeding   140, 198–9

breathing *see also* respiration

    disorders   168–9

    mechanism   167–8

C

cancer   75–6

capillaries   143

carbohydrates   7–8

carbon cycle   18

carbon dioxide (CO2)

    and global warming   18

    in photosynthesis   53–4

catabolism   11

cell

    cycle   72–3

    diversity   39–42

    division   71–6

    structure   34–8

    ultrastructure   36–7

central nervous system   173–5

chloroplasts   37

chromosomes   71

circulation, double   145–6

circulatory systems   141–3

    closed   142

    double   145–6

    human   147–8

    open   141

climatic factors   13

cohesion–tension model   128

competition   21–2

conservation   25

contraception   199–200

copulation   194

Crick, Francis   91

cytoplasm   37

D

dark stage (photosynthesis)   58–9

Darwin, Charles   101

dental formula   152

diet, balanced   157

dicots   125

diffusion   67–8

digestion

    chemical   153

    physical   152, 153

digestive system   152–7

diploid cells   72

disaccharides   7

Dixon, Henry   128

DNA (deoxyribonucleic acid)   90–7

profiles 95–7

replication 93–4

structure 90–2

dormancy (seeds) 223–4

double helix 91

duodenum 154

E

ear 179–80

ecology

  definition 12

  theory 12–23

ecosystems 24–6, 27–33

  definition 12

ectotherms 159

edaphic factors 14

electron transport system 62

embryo 195–7

endocrine

  glands 182–5

  system 182–6

endospores 111

endotherms 159

energy

  carriers 52–3, 60

  flow 14

enzymes 43–51

  factors affecting enzyme action 44–6

  immobilised 49–51

eukaryotic cells 38

evolution 100–2

exam techniques x–xi

excretion 160–4

exercise

  effect on

  breathing rate 168

  effect on heart rate 148

exocrine glands 182

eye 177–9

F

fermentation 62–4

fertilisation 78, 195

fibroids 193–4

flower structure 217–18

flowering plants 122–30, 217–27

  classification 125

  fertilisation 221

  mineral and carbon dioxide uptake and transport 129

  responses in 201–3

  sexual reproduction 217–27

  structure 122–5

  water uptake 127

food

  chain 14–15

  elements 7–11

  preservation 70

  processing 114

  web 16

fossils 102

fruit 222

Fungi 108, 116–20

G

gametes 79, 188, 218–20

genetic

  code 94

  crosses 78

engineering 103–6

  screening 97

  variation 100

genetics 77–89

genotypes 78

germination 224–7

global warming 18

glue ear 180–1

grassland habitat study 27–32

H

habitat, definition 12

haploid cells 72

heart 143–8

  and lifestyle 148

  structure 143

heartbeat 146–7

heredity 78

homeostasis 158–61

hormones 182–3

  female 192

  male 189

I

ileum 156

immune system see specific defence system

immunity

  duration of 137

  induced 139–40

infertility 190, 194

inherited variations 77

insulin 186

intestine

  large 157

  small 154–6

in-vitro fertilisation 200

J

joints 211–12
Joly, John 128

K

keys, identification 29
Krebs cycle 62

L

lactation 198
lactic acid fermentation 63
larynx 166
leaves, of flowering plants 124–5
life
 characteristics 5–6
 definition 5
ligaments 211
light stage (photosynthesis) 56–8
linked genes 85
lipids 9
liver 154–5
lungs 166
lymphatic system 149–50
lymphocytes 133

M

meiosis 76
membranes 68
Mendel, Gregor 82
Mendel's laws 82–3
menstrual cycle 191–3
metabolism 6
micro-organisms 64
micropropagation 41–2
microscope, light 34–6

minerals 10–11
mitochondrion 37
mitosis 73–5
Monera 107, 109–115
monocots 125
monocytes 133
monosaccharides 7
mouth 152
muscles 213
mutagens 100
mutations 100–1

N

natural selection 101–2
nephrons 162
nerve impulses 171–2
nervous system 170–6
neurons 170–1
niche 17
nitrogen cycle 19–20
non-nuclear inheritance 89
nucleolus 37
nucleotides 90–1
nucleus 37
nutrient recycling 17–20
nutrition
 animal 151–7
 autotrophic 151
 heterotrophic 151

O

oesophagus 153
organs and organ systems 42
osmosis 68–70

P

pancreas 154, 184
parasitism 21
parathyroids 184
Parkinson's disease 176
pathogens 135–6
pharynx 165
phenotypes 78
photosynthesis 52–9
 products of 130
pituitary gland 184
placenta 196–7
plant see also flowering plants
 cells 36
 food storage organs 130
 growth regulators 203–4
 protective adaptations 207
 responses 201–7
 tissues 39–41
plasma 131, 163
platelets 133
pollination 220
pollution 24–5
population
 control 20–1
 dynamics 22
 human numbers 22–3
portal system 147
predation 21
pregnancy 194–5
prokaryotic cells 38
propagation, vegetative 228–30
protein synthesis 98–9

proteins 8 9
Protoctista (Protists) 107
pyramid of numbers 16–17

Q

quadrats 30

R

red blood cells 132
reflex action 175
reproductive systems, human
    male 187–90
    female 190–200
respiration 60–6
    aerobic 61–2
    anaerobic 62–4
respiratory system 165–9
Rhesus factor 134
Rhizopus 117
RNA (ribonucleic acid) 98–9
roots, of flowering plants 122–3
    water uptake by 127

S

scientific method 1–4
seeds 221–4

senses 177–81
sex
    determination 81
    linkage 87
sheep's heart, dissection and display 144–5
shoots, of flowering plants 124
skeleton 208–13
    axial 209
    appendicular 209–10
skin 159–60
species 77
specific defence system (immune system) 136–7
spinal cord 174
stems, of flowering plants 124
sterilisation 119
stimulus 201
stomach 153
symbiosis 21
synapse 172–3

T

T-cells 138–9
temperature regulation, in humans 159–60
tendons 211

thyroid 185
thyroxine 185–6
tissue culture 41–2
trachea 166
transpiration 128–9
tropisms 202–3

U

urea 161
urinary system 161–4

V

valves (in veins) 143, 144
veins 142
viruses 214–16
vitamins 10

W

Wallace, Alfred Russel 101
waste management 25–6
Watson, James 91
water, importance for living things 11
white blood cells 132

Y

yeast 64, 118–19

STUDY GUIDE

Date:

Time:

Section to
be revised:

Date:

Time:

Section to
be revised:

Date:

Time:

Section to
be revised:

Date:

Time:

Section to
be revised:

Date:

Time:

Section to
be revised:

Date:

Time:

Section to
be revised:

Night before exam:

Sections to be revised:

STUDY GUIDE

Date:

Time:

Section to
be revised:

Date:

Time:

Section to
be revised:

Date:

Time:

Section to
be revised:

Date:

Time:

Section to
be revised:

Date:

Time:

Section to
be revised:

Date:

Time:

Section to
be revised:

Night before exam:

Sections to be revised:

STUDY GUIDE

Date:

Time:

Section to
be revised:

Date:

Time:

Section to
be revised:

Date:

Time:

Section to
be revised:

Date:

Time:

Section to
be revised:

Date:

Time:

Section to
be revised:

Date:

Time:

Section to
be revised:

Night before exam:

Sections to be revised:

STUDY GUIDE

Date:

Time:

Section to
be revised:

Date:

Time:

Section to
be revised:

Date:

Time:

Section to
be revised:

Date:

Time:

Section to
be revised:

Date:

Time:

Section to
be revised:

Date:

Time:

Section to
be revised:

Night before exam:

Sections to be revised: